Classic Fish

Members' Best Recipes

MINNETONKA, MINNESOTA

Classic Fish
Members' Best Recipes

Tom Carpenter
Creative Director

Jennifer Weaverling
Michele Teigen
Senior Book Development Coordinators

Phil Aarrestad
Commissioned Photography

Ron Essex
John Keenan
Assistant Photographers

Cindy Ojczyk
Food Stylist

Susan Hammes
Prop Stylist and Assistant Food Stylist

Circus Design
Book Design and Production

Guy Harvey Research Institute
Virgil Beck
Maynard Reece
Al Agnew
Wild Wings
Illustration

Special Thanks To:
NAFC members for their contributions
Bob Arndt / Brad Leuthner / Erwin Fier

Special Note: The North American Fishing Club proudly presents this special cookbook edition which includes the personal favorites of your fellow members. Each recipe has been screened by a cooking professional and edited for clarity. However, we are not able to kitchen-test these recipes and cannot guarantee their outcome, or your safety in their preparation or consumption. Please be advised that any recipes which require the use of dangerous equipment (such as pressure cookers), or potentially unsafe preparation procedures (such as canning and pickling) should be used with caution and safe, healthy practices.

6 7 8 9 10 / 09 08 07 06 05
© 2000 North American Fishing Club
ISBN 1-58159-113-6

North American Fishing Club   12301 Whitewater Drive   Minnetonka, MN 55343
www.fishingclub.com

Table of Contents

Favorites

Bill's Deep-Fried Fillets

Bill's Deep-Fried Fillets

2 cups flour

1 (12-oz.) can beer

2 eggs, beaten

2 T. salt

2 T. vinegar

¼ tsp. pepper

¼ tsp. parsley flakes

⅛ tsp. paprika

1 tsp. lemon juice

2 lbs. skinless fillets,
    cut into bite-size pieces

In large mixing bowl, combine flour, beer, eggs, salt, vinegar, pepper, parsley, paprika and lemon juice; mix until well blended. In heavy skillet, heat oil over medium-high heat until hot. Dredge fillets in batter; drop in skillet. Fry fillets until golden brown.

Bill Fett
Cascade, MT

Favorites

Batter-Fried Fish

1 lb. fish fillets

Oil

½ cup milk

1 egg

½ cup flour

¼ tsp. salt

Dash hot pepper sauce

Cut fillets into serving-size pieces. In heavy skillet, heat oil over medium-high heat until hot. In large mixing bowl, beat milk and egg. Add flour, salt and hot sauce; beat until smooth. Dip fish in batter, draining off excess. Fry 3 to 4 minutes, or until golden brown and fillets flake easily with fork. Drain on paper towels. Serve with tartar sauce.

Eugene Starkey
McMinnville, TN

Barbecued Beer Bites

6 to 8 (10-inch)
   wooden skewers
1/4 cup butter
1 T. olive oil
5 cloves garlic, crushed
1/4 tsp. onion flakes
1/4 tsp. dill weed
1/4 tsp. salt
1/4 tsp. pepper
1/2 cup beer
1 1/2 lbs. skinless fillets,
   cut into long strips

Soak skewers in water. In saucepan, combine butter, olive oil, garlic, onion flakes, dill, salt and pepper; heat and mix well. Cool and blend in beer. Skewer fillet strips and marinate in mixture in refrigerator 8 hours, turning occasionally. Spray grate of grill with nonstick spray. Place skewers on grate 3 minutes; turn and cook an additional 2 to 3 minutes.

Bill Fett
Cascade, MT

Favorites

Broiled Fillets Mexicali

2 lbs. skinless fish fillets
1 (4-oz.) can chopped
   green chiles (jalapeños may
   be substituted)
2 T. vegetable oil
2 T. soy sauce
2 T. Worcestershire sauce
1 tsp. paprika
1/2 tsp. chili powder
1/2 tsp. garlic powder
Dash hot pepper sauce

Cut fillets into serving-size portions and place in a single layer in well-greased baking dish. Combine chiles, oil, soy sauce, Worcestershire sauce, paprika, chili powder, garlic powder and hot pepper sauce; pour mixture over fillets. Broil approximately 4 inches from source of heat 5 minutes or until fillets are opaque or flake with a fork. Baste once with natural juices during broiling.

John Peterie
Plano, TX

Fish in Lemon Sauce

1 1/2 lbs. fish fillets
Juice of lemon
2 T. vegetable oil
2 medium onions, chopped
1/2 tsp. salt
1/8 tsp. white pepper
1/2 cup water
Grated rind of lemon
1/4 tsp. turmeric
1/4 cup lemon sauce
1 T. cornstarch
1/4 cup plain yogurt
Parsley

Rinse and pat fillets dry. Sprinkle lemon juice over fillets, and let stand 10 to 15 minutes. In heavy skillet, heat oil over medium-high heat until hot. Sauté onion until golden brown. Add fillets; brown on each side about 5 minutes. Add salt, pepper, 1/2 cup water, lemon rind, turmeric, lemon sauce and cornstarch. Simmer, covered, about 2 minutes or until thickened. Stir in yogurt; remove from heat. Garnish with parsley.

Paul H. Wells
Sierra Vista, AZ

Foiling Fish

Fish of choice
Lemon juice
Salt
Pepper
Water

Arrange fish in foil. Add lemon juice, salt and pepper. If you do not like lemon flavor, add some water to dilute it. Place foil pack on grill and cook until fish flakes easily with fork, turning once.

Adam Schmidt
Hockley, TX

9

Fillet of Fish with Basil Scallion Butter

Fillet of Fish with Basil Scallion Butter

1/2 lb. salted butter,
   room temperature
1/4 cup Dijon mustard
1/3 cup chopped fresh basil leaves
1/4 cup chopped fresh parsley
1/4 cup diced scallion tops
4 medium fish fillets, rinsed,
   patted dry
4 T. butter, melted
1/4 cup water
1 fresh tomato,
   seeded, chopped

Heat oven to 375°F. Butter 9 x 13-inch baking dish. Combine 1/2 lb. butter, mustard, basil, parsley and scallions. Cream until thoroughly blended. Set aside. Place fillets in prepared baking dish and pour melted butter and water over fillets. Bake until golden brown, or until fillets flake easily with fork. Transfer fillets to serving platter, bathing generously with seasoned butter. Sprinkle with chopped tomato.

Michael Bryan
Pollocksville, NC

Favorites

Fish & Rice

Favorite fish
Brown rice (boiled)
2 large tomatoes, chopped
1 large onion, chopped
4 T. butter, melted
Salt and pepper
Old Bay seasoning

Top fillets with rice, tomatoes and onion. Pour melted butter over fish. Bake at 350°F 20 to 30 minutes. Sprinkle with salt, pepper and seasoning.

Kathleen Wilson
McAlpin, FL

Fish Snack Supreme

3/4 lb. leftover fried or baked fish
2 T. green onions
4 T. Kraft tartar sauce
3 T. mayonnaise
3 T. horseradish
1/8 tsp. salt
1/8 tsp. pepper
1/8 tsp. cayenne
1 T. lemon juice
1 small cucumber, thinly sliced
Snack crackers

Use only white, flaky meat from fish - no breading. Finely chop fish and green onions. Add tartar sauce, mayonnaise, horseradish, salt, pepper and cayenne. Mix thoroughly. Add 1 tablespoon lemon juice. Place slice of cucumber on snack cracker. Place fish spread on top of cucumber. Top with sliced jalapeño, chopped radish and sprigs of dill, if desired.

Paul H. Wells
Sierra Vista, AZ

Caribbean Fish Broth

6 fish fillets
Garlic, salt, pepper, lime juice,
   chives and thyme
1 medium potato
2 green bananas
1 carrot
1 small onion
1 small tomato
Butter

Season fillets with garlic, salt, pepper, lime juice, chives and thyme to taste. Peel bananas, potato, carrot, onion and tomato; cut into bite-size pieces; boil. When bananas and vegetables are cooked through, add butter and fish. Add water if necessary. Serve hot.

Kalowtie Seeriram
Queens, NY

Fish Snack Supreme

Hollandaise Fillets

Hollandaise Fillets

2 lbs. boneless white fish fillets
1 (14.5-oz.) can mushrooms,
   sliced, strained
3 green onions
Salt and pepper
1/2 cup white wine
1/2 cup water
1 pkg. hollandaise mix
Lettuce
Fresh parsley
Cherry tomatoes
Paprika

Roll fish fillets and secure with toothpicks. Place in greased pan and cover with mushrooms and onions. Season with salt and pepper to taste. Pour in wine and water, cover pan and simmer 20 minutes. Meanwhile, prepare hollandaise mix according to package directions. After simmering fish, place on serving dish and drizzle with hollandaise sauce. Serve on bed of lettuce and garnish with parsley sprigs, cherry tomatoes and paprika.

John Pelrine
Chicago, IL

Gene's Sardine Smelt

1 pint jar
Olive oil
1 T. ketchup or tomato sauce
1/2 tsp. canning salt

Prepare smelt and pack in clean pint canning jar. Fill jar with olive oil to within 2 inches from top. Add ketchup and salt. Heat canning jar in hot water; seal. Put in pressure cooker; cook 30 minutes at 10 to 12 Psi.

Options:

Louisiana-Style
Add 1 teaspoon finely ground horseradish to ketchup
   (or ground cayenne to taste)

Mustard-Style
Instead of ketchup, use 1 tablespoon prepared mustard
   plus 1 teaspoon of finely ground horseradish

Eugene Spurgess
Milford, MI

Lucky's Pickled Fish

Fish fillets
4 cups water
1 cup salt
White vinegar
Onion slices
Lemon slices

*C*ut fillets into 1-inch squares. Combine water and salt. Add fillets to brine; refrigerate 48 hours. Drain and rinse. Place fillets, onion and lemon slices into jars. Can also be done in gallon glass jar or crock. Add 1 dry red bell pepper and garlic, if desired.

Brine
2 cups white vinegar
1 3/4 cups sugar
4 bay leaves
5 cloves
1 tsp. whole allspice
2 tsp. mustard seed
1 tsp. whole black pepper

*I*n Dutch oven, combine vinegar, sugar, bay leaves, garlic, and spices. Boil and cool.

Marvin Wright
Fairbanks, AK

Lucky's Pickled Fish

Pickled Fish

7 cups water
1 heaping cup pickling salt
5 lbs. fresh fish,
    cut into small pieces
White vinegar to cover fish
    plus 4 cups
3 cups sugar
1 cup white wine
1/4 cup mixed pickling spices
Onion slices

In Dutch oven, combine water and salt. Add fish; refrigerate 48 hours. Drain salted water. Cover fish with white vinegar; refrigerate 24 hours. Drain vinegar. Boil 4 cups vinegar and sugar; cool. Add wine, pickling spices and onion slices. Pour over fish and refrigerate 48 hours before serving.

Larry J. Kirschbaum
Glen Haven, WI

Quiche

3 eggs, beaten
1 (3-oz.) pkg. cream cheese
1 cup cottage cheese
1/4 cup melted butter
1/4 cup flour
1/2 tsp. baking powder
1/2 cup milk
1 cup cooked, flaked, fish
1/2 cup cooked, chopped, ham
1 cup grated cheddar cheese
Bacon

Heat oven to 350°F. In large mixing bowl, combine eggs, cream cheese, cottage cheese and butter; mix until well blended. In another mixing bowl, combine flour and baking powder. Combine dry mixture with egg mixture. Blend in milk, add fish and ham. Pour mixture into buttered pie plate; sprinkle cheddar cheese and bacon on top. Bake 30 to 40 minutes, or until center is firm.

Bill Fett
Cascade, MT

Quick Lakeside Dinner

2 T. butter or margarine

2 cups canned tomatoes,
    chopped, drained

1 cup dried celery

2 medium onions, chopped

1 1/2 lbs. fish fillets, cut into
    bite-size pieces

1 tsp. salt

1/4 tsp. black pepper

2 cups canned potatoes,
    drained, sliced

In heavy skillet, heat butter over medium-high heat until melted. Sauté tomatoes, celery and onions 3 to 5 minutes or until onions are soft. Add fillets, salt, pepper and potatoes; stir once. Cover skillet; simmer 10 minutes.

Paul H. Wells
Sierra Vista, AZ

Pan-Fried Fish

1/4 cup milk

1 egg, slightly beaten

2 lbs. dressed fish
    or 1 lb. fish fillets

1/2 cup flour

1/4 cup oil

Salt and pepper

In small mixing bowl, combine milk and egg. Dip fillets in mixture; coat with flour. In large heavy skillet, heat oil over medium-high heat until hot. Fry fillets 5 to 7 minutes, or until golden brown and fillets flake easily with fork. Turn fillets over only once; season with salt and pepper to taste.

Eugene Starkey
McMinnville, TN

Onion-Baked Fillets

Onion-Baked Fillets

2 lbs. skinless fish fillets

1/2 tsp. salt

1 cup sour cream

1 cup mayonnaise

1 (1.6-oz.) pkg. Original Ranch
  salad dressing mix

1 (6-oz.) can French fried
  onions, crushed

Cut fillets into serving-size portions. Sprinkle with salt. In mixing bowl, combine sour cream, mayonnaise and salad dressing mix; mix until well combined. Dip fillets into mixture. Roll fillets in crushed onions. Place fillets on well-greased baking pan. Bake at 375°F 10 minutes per inch of fish thickness, or until fish is opaque. Serve with remaining dressing, if desired.

John Peterie
Plano, TX

Favorites

Red Chowder

5 cups water

1 (14.5-oz.) can tomatoes

2 cloves garlic, minced

2 bay leaves

1/4 cup parsley

2 carrots, shredded

2 ribs celery, chopped

1 onion, chopped

1/2 tsp. thyme

1 T. Old Bay seasoning

2 cups favorite fish, cubed

In Dutch oven, combine water, tomatoes, garlic, bay leaves, parsley, carrots, celery, onion, thyme and seasoning salt. Add fish. Simmer 1 hour before serving.

Kathleen Wilson
McAlpin, FL

Fish Stew Provençale

2 cups clamato juice
1 (16-oz.) can sliced, stewed,
    tomatoes, undrained
2 onions, thinly sliced
2 cloves garlic, minced
2 T. olive juice (optional)
1 carrot, thinly sliced
1 or 2 bay leaves
1 tsp. fennel seeds
1/4 tsp. dried thyme
1/4 tsp. dried marjoram
Pinch saffron
Salt and pepper
1/2 cup water
1 lb. firm fish fillets, cubed
1/2 cup white wine

In Dutch oven, combine clamato juice, tomatoes, onions, garlic, carrot, bay leaves, fennel, thyme, marjoram, saffron, salt, pepper and water. Cover and simmer 20 to 25 minutes. Add fish cubes and wine. Cover and simmer an additional 5 to 10 minutes. Serve immediately.

William Picking
Monson, MA

Fishburgers

1 lb. ground fish, your choice
1 T. lemon juice
1/4 cup flour
1/2 tsp. salt
1/8 tsp. pepper
Oil
Lettuce
Mayonnaise
6 tomato slices
6 split hamburger buns, heated

In mixing bowl, combine ground fish, lemon juice, flour, salt and pepper; form mixture into patties. In heavy skillet, heat oil over medium-high heat until hot. Cook patties 8 to 10 minutes or until meat is browned on both sides. Arrange crisp lettuce, fish patty, mayonnaise and slice of tomato on hamburger bun. Serve hot.

Ronald Runyon
DuBois, PA

Fish Turbans with Newburg Sauce

2 lbs. fresh fish fillets
1 tsp. salt
1/4 tsp. pepper
1/4 cup butter, melted
2 cups cooked rice
Paprika
Parsley sprigs

Cut fillets into serving-size pieces. Sprinkle with salt and pepper. Roll into turbans; secure with toothpicks. Arrange fillets in well-greased 8 x 8 x 2-inch baking dish. Brush with butter and bake at 350°F 15 to 20 minutes, or until fish flakes easily. Meanwhile, prepare the Newburg sauce.

Newburg Sauce
1/2 cup butter
1/4 cup flour
1/2 tsp. salt
1/8 tsp. cayenne
3 cups half and half
Dash hot sauce
6 egg yolks, beaten
1/3 cup sherry

Melt butter in saucepan; stir in flour, salt and cayenne. Add half-and-half gradually; cook until thick and smooth, stirring constantly. Stir hot sauce into egg yolks; add to remaining sauce, stirring constantly. Remove from heat and add sherry.

To serve, remove toothpicks from turbans; place on bed of rice. Spoon Newburg sauce over turbans; garnish with paprika and parsley sprigs.

Paul H. Wells
Sierra Vista, AZ

To the Side

Chili Cheese Cornbread

Chili Cheese Cornbread

1 1/2 cups buttermilk pancake mix
1 cup cornmeal mix
1/2 tsp. baking powder
1/2 tsp. salt
1 tsp. chili powder
Parmesan
1/3 cup grated jalapeño cheese
1 (4-oz.) can diced green
    chili peppers
1/2 cup finely diced onions
1 egg, slightly beaten
1/2 cup milk

Heat oven to 375°F. In large mixing bowl, combine pancake mix, cornmeal mix, baking powder, salt and chili powder; mix well. Add Parmesan, jalapeño cheese, green chiles, onions, egg and milk. Stir until just combined. Pour mixture into a well-oiled baking dish. Bake 20 minutes, or until golden brown.

Jim Fain
Susanville, CA

Corn Cakes

1 1/2 cups flour
1/2 cup cornmeal
1 tsp. baking powder
1 tsp. salt
2 (3-oz.) pkgs. cream cheese, softened
6 eggs
1 cup milk
1/4 cup butter, melted
1 (12-oz.) can corn, drained
1/2 cup salsa
1/4 cup chopped green onions

In large mixing bowl, combine flour, cornmeal, baking powder and salt; mix until well blended. Beat in cream cheese and eggs. Add milk and butter. Fold in corn, salsa and onions. In heavy skillet, heat oil over medium-high heat until hot. Pour batter by 1/4 cup. Flip cakes when bubbles appear. Serve with sour cream, salsa and favorite fish.

Kathleen Wilson
McAlpin, FL

Backwoods Scallop Potatoes

4 medium potatoes, sliced
1/4 cup wild mushrooms
    or 1 small can mushrooms
    or 3 slices bacon, chopped
1 small onion
4 T. butter
1 (10 3/4-oz.) can
    broccoli cheese soup
1/3 cup milk
Pepper

In large skillet sauté potatoes, mushrooms and onion in butter. Reduce heat, add soup, milk and pepper. Cover and cook 5 to 10 minutes.

Doug Paugh
Oakland, MD

Hoppin' John

1 1/4 cups fresh
    black-eyed peas
4 cups water
2 T. chicken bouillon granules
2 jalapeño peppers, seeded,
    minced
1 small onion, finely chopped
3/4 cup white rice
Salt and pepper

In Dutch oven, combine peas, water, bouillon, jalapeños and onion; bring to a boil. Reduce heat to a slow boil and cook 10 minutes. Add rice; continue to slow boil 20 to 25 minutes. Salt and pepper to taste.

Jim Fain
Susanville, CA

Broccoli & Egg Au Gratin

1 (10³/₄-oz.) can cream
   of celery soup
²/₃ cup milk
2 (10-oz.) pkgs. broccoli spears
3 hard-boiled eggs, sliced
1 (2.8-oz.) can
   French fried onions
¹/₂ cup shredded Swiss cheese

Heat oven to 350°F. In small bowl, combine soup and milk. In 8 x 12-inch baking dish, arrange broccoli spears down center, alternating direction of florets. Layer sliced egg, ¹/₂ can French fried onions, soup mixture and cheese over broccoli stacks. Bake, covered, 25 minutes or until heated through. Top with remaining onions. Bake, uncovered, 5 minutes or until onions are golden brown.

Michael Baer
Hazard, KY

To the Side

Frankie's Cornbread

1 ¹/₂ cups cornmeal
1 ¹/₂ cups flour
1 T. baking powder
1 tsp. baking soda
1 tsp. salt
2 T. sugar
1 ¹/₂ cups mayonnaise
2 eggs, slightly beaten
³/₄ to 1 cup buttermilk

Heat oven to 325°F. Combine cornmeal, flour, baking powder, baking soda, salt and sugar; mix well. Add mayonnaise, eggs and buttermilk; beat on medium speed. Pour mixture into cold, oiled, 10-inch cast iron skillet. Bake 35 minutes or until golden brown.

Jim Fain
Susanville, CA

Hush Puppies

2 cups cornmeal
1/2 cup flour
1 tsp. baking powder
1 tsp. baking soda
1 tsp. salt
1 egg, slightly beaten
2 cups milk
1/2 cup finely chopped onion
2 jalapeños, seeded,
  minced
Dash cayenne

In a large mixing bowl, combine cornmeal, flour, baking powder, baking soda and salt; mix well. Add egg, milk, onion, jalapeño and cayenne. Heat large skillet over medium-high heat until hot. Cover bottom with 2 inches of oil; heat until 375°F. Drop teaspoon-sized mixture into oil and fry until golden brown.

Jim Fain
Susanville, CA

To the Side

Orange Potato Nuggets

Potatoes (1 large potato
  per person), peeled, diced
Grated orange rind
2 eggs, beaten
Salt and pepper
2 T. butter
2 T. milk
Flour
White cornmeal
  or fine dry bread crumbs
Oil

In Dutch oven, boil potatoes; drain and mash. Add orange rind, 1 egg, salt and pepper, butter and milk; mix thoroughly. Form potato mixture into bite-size portions and roll in flour. Brush floured nuggets with remaining 1 beaten egg and dust with cornmeal or bread crumbs. Heat oil in large skillet over medium-high heat until hot. Add nuggets; deep fry until golden brown.

Jeff Fee
Lancaster, OH

Potato Onion Dish

5 to 6 medium potatoes

4 to 6 eggs, hard boiled

1/2 cup onions
    chopped

1 head lettuce

2 cups mayonnaise

Salt and pepper

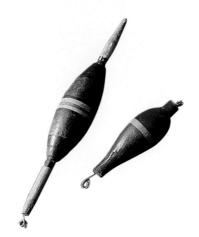

Add whole potatoes and eggs to salted water. Cook until potatoes are soft; refrigerate. Peel and cut potatoes into 3/4-inch pieces. Shell and cut eggs into small pieces. Place in large bowl and add 1/2 cup onions. Tear lettuce into pieces; add to bowl. Add mayonnaise, salt and pepper. For extra flavor, you may add 1 teaspoon celery flakes or garlic powder, or put slices of egg around top and garnish with paprika.

Frances & Ethan Freeman
Arbuckle, CA

Rich Potato Casserole

1 (2-lb.) pkg. hash
    brown potatoes, thawed

2 cups sour cream

1/2 cup chopped onion

2 cups shredded cheddar cheese

1 (10 3/4-oz.) can cream
    of mushroom soup

1/2 tsp. salt

Dash pepper

1 stick butter

2 cups slightly crushed corn flakes

Heat oven to 350°F. Grease 9 x 13-inch baking dish. Cover bottom with hash browns. In large bowl, combine sour cream, onion, cheese, soup, salt, pepper and half of melted butter; mix until well blended. Spread mixture over potatoes; top with corn flakes and drizzle with remaining butter. Bake 1 hour.

Kathleen Wilson
McAlpin, FL

Easy Fruit Cobbler

6 T. butter
1 cup flour
3/4 cup sugar
2 tsp. baking powder
3/4 cup milk
Cinnamon
Nutmeg
Pinch salt
1 (15-oz.) can sliced,
    drained, fruit

Heat oven to 375°F. In large mixing bowl, combine melted butter, flour, sugar, baking powder, milk, cinnamon, nutmeg and salt; mix well. Pour batter mixture into baking dish; top with fruit. Bake 30 minutes or until done. Serve with heavy cream or vanilla ice cream.

Jim Fain
Susanville, CA

To the Side

Fish Dressing

2 T. lemon juice
Garlic to taste
1/2 cup salad dressing
1/2 cup puréed spinach

In large mixing bowl, combine lemon juice, garlic, salad dressing and spinach; mix until well blended. Refrigerate 1 hour before serving.

Arnold McIntyre
Mayville, NY

Easy Fruit Cobbler

Scalloped Ham & Potatoes

3 lbs. potatoes, thinly sliced
3 1/4 cups milk
1/3 cup flour
1 T. chicken broth granules
1 tsp. crushed dried thyme
1/2 tsp. salt
1/4 tsp. pepper
12 oz. ham,
    thinly sliced, chopped
1/2 medium onion, thinly sliced
3/4 cup shredded Jack,
    Swiss or jalapeño cheese
Paprika

Boil sliced potatoes 3 minutes; drain and set aside. Heat oven to 375°F. Coat inside of shallow 2 1/2 - to 3-quart baking dish with nonstick cooking spray. In medium saucepan, stir together 1/2 cup of milk and flour until smooth. Stir in remaining milk, chicken granules, thyme, salt and pepper. Stir over medium heat until sauce thickens and bubbles, about 3 minutes. Add 1/3 of potatoes into baking dish. Sprinkle with 1/2 each of ham and onions. Add 1/3 of sauce. Repeat layers. Top layer should be potatoes with remaining 1/3 sauce. Bake, covered, 30 minutes. Sprinkle cheese over top and dust with paprika. Bake uncovered until lightly browned, about 15 minutes. Cool 10 to 15 minutes before serving.

Jim Fain
Susanville, CA

Seafood Dip

2 lbs. crabmeat
1/2 lb. small shrimp
1 (18-oz.) bottle
    shrimp cocktail sauce
1 lb. cream cheese

In large mixing bowl, combine crabmeat, shrimp, cocktail sauce and cream cheese; mix with hand mixer on medium speed until well mixed. Refrigerate 1 hour. Serve with crackers.

Nancy Newton
Houston, TX

White & Wild Rice Nutty Pilaf

2 cups water
1 T. chicken bouillon
1 tsp. Italian seasoning
2 cloves garlic, minced
1 cup Uncle Ben's Rice
1/3 cup wild rice
1/3 cup sliced almonds
   or chopped walnuts
2 to 3 green onions, chopped
3/4 cup sliced fresh mushrooms
Butter
Salt and pepper

In Dutch oven, combine water, chicken bouillon, Italian seasoning and garlic. Bring to a boil. Add rice; stir and cover. Reduce heat to a slow boil. Cook 10 minutes. Add nuts, onions and mushrooms; stir. Cook another 10 minutes or until liquid is absorbed. Add butter, salt and pepper to taste.

Jim Fain
Susanville, CA

To the Side

W. R. M.'s Tartar Sauce

1 cup reduced-calorie mayonnaise
1 tsp. mustard
1 tsp. finely chopped lemon peel
1 T. fresh lemon juice
Pepper
2 T. pickle relish
2 T. chopped parsley
2 T. chopped onion
Dash Tabasco sauce

In large mixing bowl, combine mayonnaise, mustard, lemon peel, lemon juice, pepper, relish, parsley, onion and Tabasco sauce; mix until well combined. Refrigerate 1 hour.

Wayne Musilek
Sturgis, SD

Seafood

Flounder
En Papillote

Flounder En Papillote

1 T. olive oil

1 cup julienne carrots

1 cup julienne snow peas

3 green onions,
   cut in 2-inch pieces

2 T. lemon juice

1/2 tsp. ground pepper

2 (8-oz.) flounder fillets,
   cut in half lengthwise

1/2 cup crumbled blue cheese

In heavy skillet, heat oil over medium-high heat until hot. Add carrots, snow peas and onions; sauté until crisp-tender. Stir in lemon juice and pepper. Remove from heat; set aside.

Cut 4 (13 x 13-inch) pieces of parchment paper; trim each into heart shape. Arrange half of vegetable mixture on half of each parchment heart. Top with 1 fillet and 2 tablespoons cheese. Fold over other half of each parchment heart starting with rounded edge; pleat and crimp edges together to seal. Twist ends tightly to seal. Place on large baking sheet. Bake at 350°F 15 to 20 minutes or until parchment is puffed and lightly browned. Place on individual serving plates; cut open. Serve immediately.

Charles Madore
Eagar, AZ

Seafood

Apple-Stuffed Fillets

1 T. oil
1/2 cup chopped onion
1/4 cup chopped parsley
1/8 tsp. crushed thyme
1 cup shredded apples
1 cup shredded carrots
2 T. lemon juice
1/4 tsp. ground ginger
1 lb. white fish fillets
1/4 cup dry white wine
Salt and pepper

In heavy skillet, heat oil over medium-high heat until hot. Sauté onion until tender. Add parsley, thyme, apples, carrots, lemon juice and ginger; sauté 3 to 4 minutes. Spread mixture evenly over length of fillets, carefully roll up. Place seam side down in oiled baking pan. Pour wine over fillets and season to taste with salt and pepper. Bake at 450°F allowing about 10 minutes cooking time per inch of thickness, measured at thickest part after stuffing. Baste once or twice during cooking.

Doug Paugh
Oakland, MD

Seafood

Crab Cakes

Meat of 2 Dungeness crabs
1 small onion, diced
1/2 cup half-and-half
1/8 tsp. cayenne
2 eggs, beaten
1 cup cracker crumbs
1/2 tsp. lemon pepper
1/4 tsp. dry mustard
2 T. butter, melted
Italian bread crumbs
Olive oil
Lemon wedges

In large mixing bowl, combine crab, onion, half-and-half, cayenne, eggs, cracker crumbs, lemon pepper, dry mustard, and butter; mix until well blended. Form mixture into patties. In heavy skillet, heat oil over medium-high heat until hot. Fry patties until golden brown on both sides. Serve with lemon wedges.

Wayne Musilek
Sturgis, SD

Grilled Shark Steak

Shark fillets
Milk
Salt
Olive oil
Garlic
Salt and pepper
Seasoning salt
Lemon, sliced

In large resealable plastic bag, freeze fillets with milk and salt solution 8 to 12 hours. Remove from freezer and allow to thaw slowly. Once thawed, pat each steak dry with towel, then rub steak down with generous amount of olive oil. Place steaks in large container with plenty of your favorite grillable vegetables. Generously season with your favorite seasonings. Recommended seasonings are garlic, salt, pepper, Everglades seasoning and something spicy. Make sure all areas of steak are covered. Add plenty of fresh lemon. Refrigerate until ready to grill. Grill steaks over hot coals until meat is white in center.

Brandon Bossard
Fort Myers, FL

Lobster Tails

¹/₄ cup butter
1 clove garlic, crushed
¹/₂ tsp. salt
1 tsp. pepper
2 tsp. paprika
4 to 6 lobster tails

In heavy skillet, heat butter over medium-high heat until melted. Stir in garlic, salt, pepper and paprika; sauté 2 to 3 minutes. Meanwhile, cut tails open along top side, lengthwise, just to tips. Pull open and place on a 9 x13-inch baking sheet. Pour butter mixture over tails. Bake at 400°F 30 to 45 minutes.

Nancy Newton
Houston, TX

Four-Bean Salad with Tuna

1 (14-oz.) can garbanzo beans

1 (14-oz.) can cannellini beans

1 (14-oz.) can red beans

1 (14-oz.) can black-eyed peas

6 T. French dressing

1 large clove garlic, minced

4 ribs celery, trimmed,
   cut into 1/4-inch-wide slices

1 medium red onion, peeled,
   chopped

Salt and pepper

1 (7-oz.) can tuna

3 hard-boiled eggs, cooled,
   shelled, quartered

Seafood

Drain beans in colander and rinse under cold running water. Line 9 x 13-inch baking sheet with double layer of paper towels. Spread beans on paper towels and shake tray until beans are no longer wet. Pour dressing into large bowl, add beans, garlic, celery, onion, salt and pepper and toss well. Break tuna into large chunks and add to bean mixture. Cover and chill 4 hours. Garnish with hard-boiled eggs.

Anthony G. Andrews Jr.
Lebanon, NH

Fish at Its Easiest

1 lb. flounder fillets

1 (10 3/4 -oz.)
   can cream of celery soup

1/2 cup grated cheese

Heat oven to 350°F. In shallow baking pan, cover fillets with soup; top with cheese. Bake 20 minutes or until tender.

Joseph Sannino
Petersburg, NJ

Four-Bean Salad with Tuna

Poor Man's Lobster

Poor Man's Lobster

1 lb. butter, melted
4 cloves garlic, minced
Salt
Dash hot pepper sauce
3 T. fresh lemon juice
1 (2- to 3-lb.) monk fillet,
    quartered

In saucepan, combine butter, garlic, salt, hot pepper sauce and lemon juice; simmer. Meanwhile, broil or steam fillet until flaky. Pour butter mixture into 4 small bowls for dipping. Serve with rice pilaf or baked potato and favorite vegetable.

Jim Fain
Susanville, CA

Seafood

Crab-Stuffed Squid

2 dozen small squid tubes
1 1/2 lbs. crabmeat, cooked, shelled
1 1/2 cups flour,
    seasoned with salt and pepper
Oil
Tempura Batter

Stuff squid tubes with crabmeat. In large saucepan, heat oil over medium-high heat until hot. Coat squid with flour mixture. Dip squid in tempura batter; deep fry until golden brown. Serve with ranch dressing dip or other favorite.

Tempura Batter
1 cup flour
2 T. cornstarch
1/2 tsp. salt
1 cup ice water
1 egg yolk
2 egg whites, beaten

In large mixing bowl, combine flour, cornstarch and salt; mix well. Add water and egg yolk; stir until just mixed. Fold in egg whites gently. Use immediately.

Jim Fain
Susanville, CA

Hot Fish Mousse

Butter
1 lb. fish (shad, salmon, sole,
    flounder, haddock)
4 egg whites
1 cup heavy cream
1 tsp. salt
1/8 tsp. powdered mace

Heat oven to 350°F. Grease 6 custard cups. Fill a shallow pan half full of hot water. In food processor, process fish until creamy. In chilled bowl set in ice water, whip egg whites and cream with salt and mace; blend into fish mixture. Pour mixture into small molds, filling each about two-thirds full. Cover tops with buttered wax paper. Set molds in pan of hot water and bake 20 to 25 minutes.

Thomas Reece
Herculaneum, MO

Seafood

Savory Fish Chowder

2 T. oil
1 medium onion, sliced
1 medium green pepper, diced
1 clove garlic, minced
4 medium tomatoes,
    cut into eighths
1/2 cup dry white wine
1/2 tsp. oregano leaves
1 small bay leaf
Pepper
2 T. parsley, minced
1/2 tsp. thyme
1 (16-oz.) pkg. frozen fish,
    thawed

In 3-quart saucepan, heat oil over medium-high heat until hot. Sauté onion, green pepper and garlic about 5 minutes, or until tender. Stir in tomatoes, white wine, oregano, bay leaf, pepper, parsley and thyme; Heat to boiling. Reduce heat to low, cover and simmer 5 minutes. Cut fish in half lengthwise, then each half into 12 pieces. Add to tomato mixture and heat to boiling. Reduce heat and cook until done. Remove bay leaf.

Arnold McIntyre
Mayville, NY

Herb-Crusted Fish

1 (15-oz.) can dry bread crumbs
2 T. chopped mixed fresh
  tarragon, dill and chervil
1 lemon rind, grated
4 haddock fillets,
  1/4 lb. each, skinned
Salt and pepper
2 T. flour
1 egg, beaten
2 T. olive oil
Juice from 1 lemon

In food processor, combine bread crumbs, herbs and lemon rind; process. Sprinkle fillets with salt and pepper, then coat with flour and shake off excess. Dip each fillet in beaten egg, coat with crumb mixture. In heavy skillet, heat oil over medium-high heat until hot. Add fillets and cook 3 minutes on each side, or until golden brown and crisp. Serve hot, with juice squeezed from lemon.

Anthony G. Andrews Jr.
Lebanon, NY

Grilled Mahi with Arugula

1 (4 oz.) mahi mahi steak
2 tsp. olive oil
1 purple onion, thinly sliced
2 cloves garlic
Salt
Pepper
2 tomatoes, peeled,
  seeded, chopped
1 handful chopped fresh arugula
  (or watercress)

Rinse steak and pat dry. Brush steak with 1 teaspoon oil; grill over medium-hot coals. Use remaining 1 teaspoon oil to coat bottom of skillet. Sauté onion and garlic with salt and pepper until onion is translucent and garlic has begun to color. Add tomatoes; cook until tomatoes glisten. Add arugula, tossing to blend. Adjust salt and pepper, serve over grilled fish.

Karen Mintzias
Via Internet

Pignant-Broiled Halibut

1 cup plain, low-fat yogurt

2 tsp. curry powder

1 tsp. dried tarragon

1 tsp. gingerroot,
  peeled, minced

1/4 tsp. salt

1 clove garlic, minced

2 T. lemon juice

8 halibut steaks or fillets

1/8 tsp. pepper

1 green bell pepper,
  cut in rings

8 cherry tomatoes, halved

In large mixing bowl, combine yogurt, curry, tarragon, ginger, salt, garlic and 1 tablespoon lemon juice in bowl; mix until well blended, set aside.

Place halibut on broiler rack coated with nonstick cooking spray. Sprinkle with pepper and remaining 1 tablespoon lemon juice; top each with pepper ring. Broil 4 to 5 inches from heat, 6 to 7 minutes, or until halibut flakes easily. Transfer halibut to serving platter; top with tomato halves and serve with sauce.

Charles Madore
Eagar, AZ

Crawfish Étouffée

1 pkg. Cajun-style rice

1 1/2 qts. water

2 T. butter

2 tsp. salt

1 1/2 cups vegetable oil

2 cups flour

1/2 cup tomato paste

2 qts. seafood stock

1/4 cup sliced green onions
(optional)

2 lbs. crawfish tails,
  cooked, peeled

In medium saucepan, combine rice, water, butter and salt in saucepan; bring to boil. Remove from heat, cover and let stand. Heat oil in stockpot; add flour, stir to combine until color is dark mahogany. Stir in tomato paste. Gradually add stock, stirring occasionally. Reduce heat and simmer 5 minutes. Add onions and crawfish and simmer an additional 5 minutes. Ladle 4 ounces over 1/2 cup of hot, cooked rice.

Charles Madore
Eagar, AZ

Microwave-Breaded Fish

1 lb. thick white fish fillets
1/4 cup reduced-calorie
 mayonnaise or salad dressing
1 tsp. lemon juice
Dash garlic powder,
 pepper and paprika
8 butter-flavored crackers,
 crushed (or enough
 to bread fish)

Coat 2-quart microwavable dish with nonstick cooking spray. Cut fish into serving-size pieces. Pat dry. In small bowl, blend mayonnaise or salad dressing, lemon juice, garlic powder, pepper and paprika until smooth. Spread evenly over fish. Sprinkle with crushed crackers. Microwave, uncovered, 4 to 5 minutes at highest power or until fish flakes easily with fork. Rotate dish after two minutes. Serve immediately.

J. Frank Jackson
Newark, OH

Orange Ruffie

8 eggs
Curry powder
1/2 cup milk
2 red ruffie fillets
Lemon
Pepper
Hungarian paprika

In large mixing bowl, combine eggs, curry powder and milk; beat at high speed. Dust fillets with curry before combining with egg mixture. Refrigerate overnight; rotate fillets every six hours until ready to broil the following evening, keeping dish covered. Heat broiler to 250°F. Place filets on broiler pan and season with lemon, pepper and paprika. Place thin lemon slices on fillets and brown at 300°F 3 to 5 minutes.

Van Leer Hoffman
Hudgins, VA

Scallop Montarde

2 cups julienne zucchini

2 T. vegetable oil

1 lb. sea scallops, halved

1 1/2 cups water

2 T. Dijon mustard

2 tsp. lemon juice

1 1/2 T. cornstarch

3 T. coarsely chopped cashews

Steam zucchini; cover over boiling water until tender. Remove from heat, keep warm. In a wok, heat oil. Add half of scallops; stir-fry for 2 to 3 minutes. Remove scallops. Repeat with remaining scallops.

In small bowl, combine water, mustard, lemon juice and cornstarch; add to wok. Cook and stir until thick and bubbly.

For each serving, arrange one-fourth of zucchini on serving plate. Top with one-fourth each of scallops and sauce. Sprinkle with cashews. Serve with hot rice.

Charles Madore
Eagar, AZ

Seafood

Seafarer's Dinner

2 cups sliced potatoes,
    1/4 inch thick

1 cup sliced carrots,
    1/4 inch thick

1 medium onion, chopped

1 lb. cod, thawed,
    drained, cubed

1/2 tsp. dill weed

1/2 tsp. salt

1/8 tsp. pepper

1/4 cup butter

Heat oven to 425°F. In 1 1/4-quart covered round casserole dish, layer half each of potatoes, carrots, onion and cod. Sprinkle with 1/4 teaspoon dill weed, 1/4 teaspoon salt and 1/16 teaspoon pepper. Dot with half of butter. Repeat process with remaining ingredients. Cover and bake 45 to 50 minutes, or until vegetables are tender.

Martin Hobbs
Watertown, WI

Scallop Montarde

Stuffed Cod Fillets

Stuffed Cod Fillets

1 lb. crabmeat, (flaked)
¹/₄ cup mayonnaise
1 egg
Old Bay seasoning
¹/₂ cup bread crumbs
2 bunches green onions, chopped
2 cod fillets, 1 lb. each
1 medium tomato, sliced
4 oz. Parmesan cheese,
  freshly grated

In large mixing bowl, combine crabmeat, mayonnaise, egg, seasoning, bread crumbs and 1 bunch of chopped green onions; mix until well blended. Lightly grease baking dish and cover bottom with remaining bunch of chopped green onions. Place 1 large cod fillet on top of onions. Spread crab stuffing mixture over cod. Place second cod fillet over top of crab stuffing. Cover entire top of cod fillet with tomato slices. Cover with foil and bake 45 minutes at 350°F. Remove foil and smother with cheese; bake, uncovered 15 minutes or until cheese is melted. Serve with wild rice.

Timothy Lisberg, Jr.
Rochester, NY

Snapper Dijon

Red snapper fillets, ¹/₄ lb. each
¹/₄ cup Dijon mustard
1 T. vinegar
¹/₂ tsp. dried whole thyme
¹/₄ tsp. pepper
Dash ground ginger
1 medium tomato, chopped
Fresh thyme sprigs

Cut four, 15-inch pieces of heavy-duty aluminum foil. Rinse fillets with cold water; pat dry. Arrange fillets just off-center on foil. In large mixing bowl, combine mustard, vinegar and dry ingredients, mix well. Pour mixture evenly over fillets. Top with tomatoes.

Fold foil over fillets and secure. Place on baking sheet. Bake at 450°F 10 minutes or until fish flakes easily. Remove fillets from foil. Garnish with thyme sprigs.

Charles Madore
Eagar, AZ

Halibut Steaks
with Almond Sauce

3 T. butter, divided
1/2 cup slivered almonds
Halibut steaks
Salt and pepper
Flour
1/2 cup milk
1 cup sour cream
1/2 cup finely chopped
   green onions
Lemon juice
Toasted almonds

Heat oven to 450°F. Lightly butter shallow baking dish large enough to hold halibut steaks in one layer. Spread almond slivers on baking sheet and toast in oven 5 minutes. Set aside to cool. Reduce oven temperature to 375°F. Melt 1 tablespoon butter in small saucepan. Brush steaks with melted butter and season with salt and pepper. Bake 20 minutes. Melt remaining 2 tablespoons butter in medium saucepan over medium heat. Add flour and cook 2 minutes, stirring constantly. Gradually add milk and continue stirring until mixture thickens. Remove from heat and stir in sour cream, onions, lemon juice and toasted almonds. Transfer halibut steaks to serving platter. Pour sauce over steaks and serve.

John Pelrine
Chicago, IL

Crab Salad

1 1/4 lbs. crabmeat, cooked, chopped
1/2 cup mayonnaise
1/2 T. lemon juice
2 to 3 ribs celery, chopped
3 to 4 green onions, chopped
1/4 medium red bell pepper, chopped
3/4 tsp. dill weed
3/4 tsp. horseradish

In medium mixing bowl, combine crabmeat, mayonnaise, lemon juice, celery, onions, pepper, dill and horseradish; mix until well blended. Refrigerate 1 hour. Serve as an appetizer or as a side dish.

Jim Fain
Susanville, CA

Halibut Supreme

Halibut fillets
White wine
Italian bread crumbs
Olive oil
Lemon pepper
Sliced onion, mushrooms,
    green peppers
Mayonnaise
Sour cream
Paprika

Cut fish into 1- to 1¹/2-inch cubes; soak in white wine overnight. Drain, roll in bread crumbs. Put drained halibut in baking pan greased with olive oil; season with lemon pepper. Top with sliced onion, mushrooms and green peppers. Cover with equal parts of mayonnaise and sour cream. Sprinkle with paprika. Bake, uncovered, at 400°F 20 to 30 minutes, or until lightly browned.

Wayne Musilek
Sturgis, SD

Halibut-Crab Delight

4 T. butter, melted
2 to 3 lbs. halibut fillets,
    cut 1 to 2 inches thick
Meat of 1 crab
Lemon pepper
Sliced onions and mushrooms
Half-and-half
Mayonnaise
1 (10³/4-oz.) can
    cream of celery soup
Paprika

Heat oven to 400°F. Pour melted butter over fillets in baking dish; spread crabmeat over fillets. Season with lemon pepper. Add onions, mushrooms, half-and-half, mayonnaise and soup. Sprinkle with paprika. Bake, uncovered, 30 minutes or until light brown.

Wayne Musilek
Sturgis, SD

Red Snapper Vera Cruz

Seafood

3 T. olive oil

1 small onion, diced

2 lbs. tomatoes,
    coarsely chopped

3 cloves garlic, minced

1/4 cup canned tomato purée

1/3 cup minced parsley

1 1/2 T. red wine vinegar

1 T. sugar

1 bay leaf

1/2 tsp. ground marjoram

1/2 tsp. ground oregano

1/2 tsp. ground thyme

1/2 tsp. pepper

1/2 tsp. salt

1/3 cup water

1/6 lb. green olives,
    cut in half

3 T. small capers

3 T. pickled jalapeños, sliced

1 1/2 T. lemon juice

2 lbs. red snapper

Flour

3 T. butter

In Dutch oven, heat olive oil in saucepan over medium-high heat until hot. Sauté onions until translucent. Add chopped tomatoes, garlic, tomato purée, parsley, vinegar, sugar, bay leaf, marjoram, oregano, thyme, pepper, salt and water. Cook 10 minutes. Add olives, capers, jalapeños and lemon juice; remove from heat. Dredge snapper in flour. In heavy skillet, heat butter over medium-high heat until melted. Sauté in butter over medium-high heat until golden brown and cooked through. Pour 1 cup of sauce over snapper and serve immediately.

Ray Sewalt
Fort Worth, TX

Haddock

3 lbs. haddock

1 qt. water

2 tsp. vinegar

2 tsp. salt

In Dutch oven, combine haddock, water, vinegar and salt; boil 30 minutes or until fish is tender.

Arnold McIntyre
Mayville, NY

Red Snapper Vera Cruz

Stuffed Flounder

1 (3-oz.) can chopped mushrooms
1/4 cup butter
1/4 cup chopped onion
1 (7-oz.) can crabmeat, drained
1/2 cup dry bread crumbs
2 T. dried parsley
Salt and pepper
2 lbs. flounder fillets
3 T. butter
3 T. flour
Milk
1/3 cup dry white wine
1 cup shredded Swiss cheese
Paprika

Drain mushrooms and reserve liquid. In heavy skillet, heat butter over medium-high heat until melted. Sauté onion about 3 minutes, or until tender. Stir in drained mushrooms, flaked crab, bread crumbs, parsley, salt and pepper. In baking dish arrange fillets. Spread mixture over fillets. Fold fillets over filling, tucking ends under. Secure with toothpicks.

Meanwhile, melt 3 tablespoons butter, stir in flour. Add 3/4 cup milk to mushroom liquid. In saucepan, combine mixture and wine. Cook and stir until sauce is thick and bubbly. Spread over fish and bake at 400°F, uncovered, about 30 minutes. Remove from oven and sprinkle with Swiss cheese and paprika. Return to oven and bake an additional 5 minutes, or until cheese melts.

John Pelrine
Chicago, IL

Golden Fish & Chips

1 1/2 lbs. haddock fillets, defrosted
2 eggs, separated
2/3 cup beer
1 cup flour
1/2 tsp. paprika
1/2 tsp. salt
2 T. butter, melted, cooled
   slightly
Oil

Cut fish into strips 3 inches long and 1 1/2 inches wide. Dry on paper towels. In large mixing bowl, beat egg yolks until thick and lemon colored. Stir in beer; add flour, paprika, salt and melted butter. Stir until smooth. Beat egg whites until stiff and fold into batter. In heavy skillet, heat oil over medium-high heat until hot. Fry fillets 2 to 3 minutes, turning occasionally. Drain on paper towels before serving.

Arnold McIntyre
Mayville, NY

Seafood & Noodles

1/2 cup butter, melted
1 small onion, chopped
1/4 green bell pepper, chopped
1 to 2 cloves garlic, minced
1 small jar chopped pimiento
   (can substitute 1/4 red
   pepper, chopped)
1 T. parsley
Pinch basil
Pepper
Dash Tabasco sauce
1 (10 3/4 oz.) can cream
   of mushroom soup
1 cup half-and-half
1 (8-oz.) pkg. imitation crabmeat
Yolk-free noodles

In Dutch oven, heat butter over medium-high heat until hot. Sauté onion, green pepper and garlic. Stir in pimiento, parsley, basil, pepper and Tabasco. Blend in soup and half-and-half. Cook 2 to 3 minutes; add crabmeat; simmer. Cook noodles according to package directions. Arrange noodles on 2 or 3 plates. Pour crab mixture over noodles.

Everett M. Trimble
Fremont, IN

Crabby Mushrooms

1 (8-oz.) pkg. cream cheese, softened
1/4 cup shredded mozzarella cheese
1/2 cup crabmeat
1 tsp. seasoning salt
10 large mushrooms

Heat oven to 350°F. In large mixing bowl, combine cream cheese, mozzarella cheese, crab and seasoning salt; mix well until blended. Remove mushroom stems and generously fill caps with cream cheese mixture. Arrange stuffed mushrooms on baking sheet. Bake 10 minutes or until cheese is melted. Serve hot.

James Morris
Marysville, WA

Walleye & Pike

Crunchy-Fried Walleye

Crunchy-Fried Walleye

1 egg
1 cup evaporated milk
2 cups cracker crumbs
1/8 tsp. salt
1/8 tsp. pepper
1 1/2 lbs. walleye, cut into 1/2-inch-
    thick slices
2 to 4 T. vegetable oil

In large mixing bowl, whisk egg and milk together; mix well. In another large mixing bowl, combine cracker crumbs, salt and pepper. Dip walleye in milk and coat with cracker crumbs. In heavy skillet, heat oil over medium-high heat until hot. Fry walleye 5 to 6 minutes or until golden brown on both sides, turning once. Drain on paper towels.

Eugene Starkey
McMinnville, TN

Camp-Cooked Walleye

1 lb. walleye fillets
1 T. lemon juice
2 tsp. butter, softened
1 tsp. dried basil
1 tsp. lemon pepper
1/2 tsp. garlic salt
4 oz. fresh mushrooms, sliced

Coat 18-inch piece of heavy aluminum foil with nonstick cooking spray and arrange fillets; sprinkle with lemon juice, butter, basil, lemon pepper and garlic salt. Top with mushroom slices. Fold and seal foil tightly over fillets. Grill, covered, over medium to hot coals 5 to 7 minutes. Turn and grill an additional 5 to 7 minutes, or until fish flakes easily with a fork.

J. Frank Jackson
Newark, OH

Baked Walleye with Vegetable Dressing

2²/₃ cups dry bread crumbs or
　croutons
1 T. snipped or dried parsley
1¹/₂ T. lemon juice
1 egg, beaten
¹/₄ tsp. pepper
3 to 4 lbs. fresh walleye fillets
¹/₂ cup chopped fresh mushrooms
³/₄ cup shredded carrots
Salt

Vegetable Dressing Mix
1 medium onion, chopped
¹/₄ cup chopped green bell pepper
¹/₄ cup chopped celery
¹/₄ cup butter, melted

Heat oven to 350°F. In large mixing bowl, combine bread crumbs, parsley, lemon juice, egg and pepper; mix until well blended. Dip fillets in mixture; drain excess. Arrange fillets in well-greased baking dish. Top with mushrooms and shredded carrots. Sprinkle with salt. Cook 30 minutes or until fish flakes with fork.

Meanwhile, in another mixing bowl combine onion, green pepper, celery and butter. Set aside. Pour over baked walleye.

John Pelrine
Chicago, IL

Walleye

1 box Stove Top Stuffing mix
6 walleye fillets
Lemon pepper
1 stick butter, melted

Heat oven to 350°F. Prepare Stove Top Stuffing according to package directions. Place stuffing in each fillet; wrap and secure with toothpick. Place on broiler pan; sprinkle with lemon pepper and melted butter. Bake 15 to 18 minutes or until walleye flakes easily.

Ray Rohde
Fargo, ND

Crispy Fish

1/2 cup mashed potato flakes
1/2 cup bread crumbs
3/4 lb. walleye
Egg substitute,
    equivalent to 1 egg
2 T. oil

In large mixing bowl, combine potato flakes and bread crumbs. Dip fish in egg substitute, then in potato mixture. In a large saucepan, heat oil over medium-high heat until hot. Cook fillet 4 to 5 minutes or until golden brown.

Keith Ratcliff
Billings, MT

Baked Walleye-Lake Erie Style

1 (3- to 4-lb.) walleye
    (dressed weight)
Salt and pepper
4 strips bacon
1 T. butter
1 clove garlic, minced
1 medium onion, sliced
1 (15-oz.) can peeled
    plum tomatoes,
    drained (reserve juice)
Dash cayenne
1 lemon, sliced thin

Heat oven to 400°F. Sprinkle fish with salt and pepper; lay in roaster on bacon strips. Add water, cover tightly and steam 10 minutes in oven. Reduce temperature to 325°F. Meanwhile, in heavy skillet, heat butter over medium-high heat until melted; sauté garlic, onion and tomatoes. Add cayenne and reserved tomato juice. Bring to boil and pour over fish. Cover fish with lemon slices and cook, uncovered, 45 minutes.

John Pelrine
Chicago, IL

Italian-Grilled Walleye

6 (8-oz.) walleye fillets
1 (16-oz.) bottle
  Italian salad dressing
1 ($10^3/4$-oz.) can tomato soup
$3/4$ cup sugar
$3/4$ cup vegetable oil
$1/3$ cup vinegar
$3/4$ tsp. celery seed
$3/4$ tsp. salt
$3/4$ tsp. pepper
$3/4$ tsp. ground mustard
$1/2$ tsp. garlic powder

In resealable plastic bag, combine fillets and salad dressing. Seal bag and refrigerate 1 hour, turning once. Combine remaining ingredients as basting sauce. Place fillets in well-greased, hinged wire basket and grill, covered, over medium coals 3 minutes on each side, basting with sauce often. Continue grilling 8 to 10 minutes, turning once and basting with sauce. Cook until fillets flake easily with a fork.

J. Frank Jackson
Newark, OH

Walleye & Pike

Walleye Salad

1 lb. walleye, poached,
  flaked
1 rib celery, sliced
1 medium onion, diced
$1/2$ tsp. hot pepper sauce
1 cup sweet pickle relish
1 cup Miracle Whip
Salt and pepper

In large mixing bowl, combine fish, celery, onion, hot pepper sauce, relish and Miracle Whip; mix until well combined. Sprinkle with salt and pepper to taste. Refrigerate mixture one hour before serving with snack crackers.

Lewis Mosier
Sherwood, OH

Italian-Grilled Walleye

Sautéed Pickerel with Lemon Butter

Sautéed Pickerel with Lemon Butter

Pickerel fillet, boned, skinned
Milk
Flour
2 T. vegetable oil
Butter
1 1/2 tsp. lemon juice
Chopped parsley

In mixing bowl, dip fillet in milk; remove and dredge in flour. In heavy skillet, heat oil over medium-high heat until hot. Heat oven to 350°F. Place fillet in pan, flesh side down, and sauté until golden brown, turning once. Transfer fillet to oven and bake 10 minutes. In same heavy skillet, heat butter over medium high heat until melted. Add lemon juice and pinch of chopped parsley. Immediately pour butter over fish fillet.

Martin Nargi
Bridgeport, CT

Walleye & Pike

Steamed Fish Rolls

2 large fish, skinned, cut into
    4 fillets
1 cup peeled, chopped, shrimp
2 T. cornstarch
1 tsp. dry sherry
4 green onions, chopped
2 eggs, beaten with pinch salt

Arrange fillets skin side up on flat surface. In large mixing bowl, combine shrimp with cornstarch, sherry and onion; divide and equally cover fillets. In heavy skillet, cook eggs until softly scrambled. Spread equal quantities of egg over fillets. Roll up fillets, jelly-roll-fashion, folding thicker end over first. Secure with toothpicks. Arrange fillets on top of steamer and fill bottom with boiling water. Steam for 10 to 15 minutes, or until fish is cooked. Remove toothpick and serve immediately.

Russell Ward
Cordova, AL

Walleye & Pike

Walleye

2 eggs
3/4 cup milk
2 lbs. fish fillets
1 cup bread crumbs
Olive oil
Seasoning salt
Salt and pepper

In large mixing bowl, combine eggs and milk; mix until well blended. Dip fillets, one at a time, in the milk and egg mixture. Put bread crumbs in resealable plastic bag. Place dipped fish in bag of bread crumbs to coat. In heavy skillet, heat oil over medium-high heat until hot. Cook fish until golden brown. Salt and pepper to taste. *Note: If seasoned bread crumbs are used, omit seasoning salt.* Serve with stewed tomatoes, home fries and slaw.

Robert Frick
Johnstown, PA

Northern Pike in Horseradish Sauce

1 cup sour cream

3 T. milk

1 T. cream style white horseradish

2 T. lemon juice

1 tsp. capers with juice

1 tsp. dry mustard

2 T. fresh parsley

1 1/2 lbs. northern pike steaks

Salt and pepper

3 T. butter or margarine

In large mixing bowl combine sour cream, milk, horseradish, lemon juice, capers with juice, dry mustard and parsley; mix until well blended. Sprinkle pike with salt and pepper. Place fillets in nonstick baking dish. Melt butter, turning fillets to coat evenly. Pour sauce over fillets and bake uncovered at 350°F 25 minutes or until the fish flakes easily with a fork. Garnish with additional chopped parsley and thinly sliced lemon. Serve hot.

John Pelrine
Chicago, IL

Trout & Salmon

Broiled Steelhead with Asparagus Sauce

Broiled Steelhead with Asparagus Sauce

3 T. olive oil

2 T. lemon juice

Salt and pepper

2 lbs. skinless,
   boneless steelhead fillets,
   cut into 4 equal-size pieces

Asparagus Sauce

In flat plate, combine olive oil, lemon juice, salt and pepper; turn fish in mixture, set aside. Place fish on broiler pan or wire rack in heatproof baking dish. Place in oven 4 inches from heat source, leaving door slightly open. Broil 2 to 3 minutes on one side. Turn and broil 2 to 5 minutes, depending on thickness of fillets. Spoon heated asparagus sauce onto 4 warmed plates. Place 1 fillet piece on each plate on top of sauce. Garnish with finely chopped parsley, sprig of fresh basil or rosemary. Serve with Rice Pilaf and steamed fresh asparagus spears.

Trout & Salmon

Asparagus Sauce

1 T. olive oil

1 T. butter

1 T. onion, finely chopped

2 cups coarsely chopped, cooked, asparagus

1/2 cup dry white wine

1 cup chicken stock

3 T. cream

In large saucepan, heat oil over medium-high heat until hot; add butter, heat until melted. Add onions and cook until transparent. Add asparagus, wine and stock; simmer and cook 5 minutes. Add cream and cook an additional 5 minutes, stirring occasionally.

Pour mixture into food processor or blender; purée. Return mixture to saucepan and heat thoroughly. Serve with broiled steelhead.

Steve Bristol
Clarkston, WA

Pa's Trout Chowder

1 small onion, sliced

1/2 cup celery, chopped

2 T. butter

2 small zucchini (about 1/2 lb.),
   cut into 1/2-inch slices

1 (14.5-oz.) can chicken broth
   and 1 1/4 cups water; omit salt

2 cups coarsely chopped cabbage

1 (15-oz.) can drained,
   northern beans

2 T. fresh parsley

1 T. fresh lemon juice

1/2 tsp. salt

4 peppercorns

1 1/4 lbs. trout steaks,
   about 1 inch thick

Thin lemon wedges

Separate onion slices into rings. In Dutch oven, stir onion and celery in butter over medium heat until onion is tender, about 5 minutes. Add zucchini, chicken broth, cabbage, beans, parsley, lemon juice, salt and peppercorns. Heat to boiling; reduce heat. Cover and simmer, stirring occasionally, 6 to 8 minutes, or until zucchini is tender. Add fish. Simmer, stirring gently once or twice, until fish flakes easily, about 10 minutes. Garnish with lemon wedges and squeeze juice over chowder before eating.

Robert Horst
Birdsboro, PA

Broiled Lake Trout

Trout fillets
1 onion, chopped
1/2 cup brown sugar

Arrange fillets in shallow pan lined with aluminum foil. Broil fillets 8 to 10 minutes, skin side up, until milky juice appears on skin. Turn fillets over and broil an additional 8 minutes. Remove fillets from broiler and cover with mixture of chopped onion and brown sugar. Return to broiler 5 minutes. Tastes great hot or cold.

Glenn DeWitt
Grimes, IA

Trout & Salmon

Crispy Broiled Salmon

6 (6- to 8-oz.) 3/4-inch-thick
   salmon steaks
1/2 cup melted butter
1 tsp. salt
1/8 tsp. paprika
1 cup crushed Saltines
1 cup crushed potato chips
6 lemon wedges
6 parsley sprigs

Rinse and pat dry steaks. In large mixing bowl, combine butter, salt and paprika; mix until well combined. Dip steaks in mixture. In another large mixing bowl, combine Saltines and potato chips. Dip steaks in mixture. Arrange steaks on lightly greased broiler rack in broiler pan. Broil 6 inches from heat 5 minutes. Turn and broil an additional 5 to 8 minutes or until fish flakes easily with fork. Serve each steak with lemon wedge and parsley sprig.

Arlys Neuberger
Lincoln, NE

Salmon Pie

2 T. butter
1 large onion, diced
1 tsp. salt
¹/₄ tsp. pepper
1 (14-oz.) can red or pink salmon
4 large potatoes
¹/₄ cup milk
¹/₂ tsp. salt
9-inch prepared pie crust

In heavy skillet, heat butter over medium-high heat until melted; sauté onion until tender. Sprinkle with salt and pepper. Add juice from canned salmon. Simmer for 2 minutes. Remove skin and bones from salmon; add salmon to onion and juice mixture; stir until well blended. Let cool to room temperature. Peel and dice potatoes. Boil, drain, and add milk and salt. Mash until smooth. Fold salmon mixture into potatoes; place in pie plate. Bake at 400°F for 30 minutes or until golden brown.

Anthony G. Andrews Jr.
Lebanon, NY

Trout & Salmon

Cheese-Stuffed Trout

¹/₄ cup sliced fresh mushrooms
¹/₄ green or white onion,
    chopped
2 T. grated Parmesan cheese
2 lbs. whole trout, cleaned
Salt and pepper

In large mixing bowl, combine mushrooms, onion and cheese; spoon mixture into cavity of each fish. Season with salt and pepper. Secure with toothpicks. Place on lightly greased broil pan. Broil 4 to 5 inches from heat 5 to 10 minutes on each side or until fish flakes easily with fork.

Bryan Walden
Henderson, KY

Salmon Niçoise Salad

1/2 lb. new potatoes,
 scrubbed
4 (14-oz.) salmon fillets
Salt and pepper
1/2 lb. green beans, trimmed,
 halved crosswise
1 clove garlic, minced
1 T. chopped fresh parsley
1 T. shredded fresh basil
4 T. French dressing
1 head crisp lettuce
 (romaine or Boston)
1/4 cup cherry tomatoes
4 hard-boiled eggs, cooled,
 shelled, cut into wedges
1/2 cup drained black olives
2-3 scallions, trimmed,
 sliced thick

Cook potatoes in stockpot of salted boiling water 15 to 20 minutes or until tender. Grill salmon fillets 2 minutes on each side. Season with salt and pepper to taste. Meanwhile, in another stockpot of salted boiling water, cook green beans about 3 minutes. Drain in colander and rinse with cold water. Drain potatoes and leave until cool enough to handle, then slice. Let cool completely.

In large mixing bowl, add garlic and herbs to French dressing and whisk to mix. Separate lettuce leaves and arrange around edges of individual plates. Cut tomatoes in half and place with eggs and potatoes on lettuce leaves, alternating them attractively. Place 1 fillet in center of each plate and surround with olives. Scatter with scallions. Pour French dressing over each. Cover loosely and chill in refrigerator about 1 hour before serving.

Anthony G. Andrews Jr.
Lebanon, NY

Max's Grilled Teriyaki Salmon

Ma's Grilled Teriyaki Salmon

1/2 cup olive oil
1/2 cup soy sauce
1/4 cup packed brown sugar
4 cloves garlic, minced
2 T. fresh ginger, chopped
2 T. toasted sesame oil
Juice of 1/2 lime
Cracked black pepper
6 salmon steaks, cut 1 inch thick

In large casserole, whisk together olive oil, soy sauce, sugar, garlic, ginger, sesame oil, lime juice and pepper; mix well. Arrange salmon in casserole; marinate 2 hours. Spray grill with nonstick cooking spray; heat to medium-hot. Place steaks on grill, baste with marinade, close cover. Turn once after 5 minutes. Baste again; close cover. Cook 10 minutes.

William S. Brown
Juneau, AK

Trout & Salmon

Fish Patties

Vegetable oil
1 small onion, finely chopped
3 eggs
1/2 tsp. dill, mace or nutmeg
1/4 tsp. lemon pepper
1 (12-oz.) can evaporated milk
1 salmon fillet, about 4 lbs.

In heavy skillet, heat oil over medium-high heat until hot. In large mixing bowl, combine onion, eggs, dill, lemon pepper and milk; beat on medium-high speed until well-mixed. Dip fillets into mixture; drain excess. Fry fillets in oil until golden brown.

Wayne Musilek
Sturgis, SD

Salmon Log Dip

1 pint canned, baked
  or smoked fish
1 (8-oz.) pkg. cream cheese,
  softened
1/2 cup mayonnaise
1/4 cup finely chopped onion
2 T. lemon juice
Paprika
Almond slivers

In large mixing bowl, combine fish, cream cheese, mayonnaise, onion and lemon juice; shape as desired. Sprinkle with paprika and almond slivers. Refrigerate before serving.

Wayne Musilek
Sturgis, SD

Salmon Loaf

1/2 cup buttered bread crumbs
1 lb. canned salmon
Dash pepper
1 T. parsley, chopped
2 eggs, beaten
1 tsp. lemon juice
1 T. butter, melted
1/2 cup milk
1/2 tsp. salt
2 tsp. finely chopped onion

In large mixing bowl, combine bread crumbs, salmon, pepper, parsley, eggs, lemon juice, butter, milk, salt and onion; mix until well blended. Heat oven to 350°F. Pack mixture firmly into buttered 8 x 3-inch loaf pan and bake 30 to 40 minutes. Garnish with parsley sprigs.

Arlys Neuberger
Lincoln, NE

Trout Amandine

1 cup milk
1/2 cup flour
Salt and pepper
8 trout fillets
2 T. plus 1/3 cup butter
1/2 cup slivered almonds
3 T. dry white wine (optional)
6 sprigs parsley
12 lemon wedges

In heavy skillet, heat 2 tablespoons butter over medium-high heat until melted. Dip fillets in milk; dredge through seasoned flour. Brown fillets on both sides. Remove fillets and arrange on serving platter; keep warm. In another skillet, sauté almonds in 1/3 cup butter; add wine. Pour almond and wine mixture over fillets. Garnish with parsley and lemon.

John Cooksey
Bedford, Texas

Lox in Phyllo Dough with Tomato & Red Pepper Coulis

1 lb. lox, roughly chopped

1 lb. cream cheese, softened

1 T. chopped cilantro

1 T. dried tarragon

1/2 bunch chopped
   green onions

1 tsp. minced garlic

1/2 tsp. curry paste
   (Petak's or curry powder)

1/2 tsp. red pepper flakes

Pinch salt

Lime

1/2 lb. phyllo dough

1/2 cup melted butter

1/2 cup plain bread crumbs

In large mixing bowl, combine lox, cream cheese, cilantro, tarragon, green onions, garlic, curry paste, red pepper flakes, salt and lime juice; mix until well blended. Cover and refrigerate 1 hour.

Heat oven to 425°F. Lay 1 sheet of phyllo dough at a time, lightly buttering and sprinkling with bread crumbs between layers. After 3 layers, cut across width into thirds, place large spoonful (about 6 T.) of filling in lower corner and fold flag-style up to end into triangle shapes. Brush tiers and tops with butter. Arrange on serving tray sprinkled with crumbs; refrigerate 30 minutes. Bake 10 to 12 minutes until dough is golden brown and crispy. Serve with coulis.

Tomato & Red Pepper Coulis

3 ripe tomatoes, cored, quartered

1 red bell pepper, seeded, cut into 1-inch pieces

1 medium onion

Juice of 1 orange

1/2 cup white wine

Pinch saffron

Salt and pepper

Hot pepper sauce

In Dutch oven, combine tomatoes, pepper, onion, orange juice, wine and saffron; boil and simmer over low heat 10 to 15 minutes. Let cool and strain through medium-fine strainer. Pour coulis into Dutch oven and simmer until thickened. Season with salt, pepper and hot sauce, if desired.

Brian Storey
Downey, CA

Herbed Salmon Steak

Salmon steak or fillet
3/4 cup dry white vermouth
3/4 cup olive oil
1 1/2 T. lemon juice
1 T. chopped fresh thyme
   or 1 tsp. dried thyme
1 T. chopped fresh marjoram
   or 1 tsp. dried marjoram
1 T. chopped fresh sage
   or 1 tsp. rubbed sage
1 T. chopped fresh parsley
3/4 tsp. salt
1/8 tsp. pepper

Arrange salmon in casserole. In large mixing bowl, combine vermouth, olive oil, lemon juice, thyme, marjoram, sage, parsley, salt and pepper; reserving 1/3 cup. Pour remaining marinade over salmon. Marinate in refrigerator 1 hour, turning once. Grill, covered, over medium heat; brush with reserved marinade.

Scott Richmond
Martinsburg, WV

Trout & Salmon

Lemon Dill Salmon Grill

2 T. dill weed
1 tsp. garlic powder
1/4 tsp. Beau Monde seasoning
4 T. olive oil
2 T. white wine vinegar
Tarragon
Juice of 2 lemons
1 1/2 lbs. Alaska salmon steaks

In large mixing bowl, combine dill weed, garlic powder, Beau Monde seasoning, olive oil, vinegar, tarragon and lemon juice; mix until well blended. Pour mixture over salmon. Marinate in refrigerator 2 hours, turning once. Brush remaining marinade on salmon while grilling.

Max Miller
Lakewood, Co

Grilled Salmon Rolls

Salmon fillets
Butter
Dill weed
Salt
Pepper
Bacon strips

Cut each fillet to length that will create 2-inch cylinder when rolled end to end. With fillet laid flat, spread butter liberally on one side. Sprinkle with dill weed, salt and pepper to taste. Roll end to end so butter and seasoning are inside cylinder. Wrap strip of bacon around outside of roll and tie tight with string. Grill fish rolls for about 20 minutes, rotating on both ends and sides. One roll will feed one person, with salad and side pasta.

Terry Plaehn
Roberts, WI

Baked Salmon

1 box Herb and Spice
    Stovetop Dressing
1 cup melted butter
1 cup white wine
1 small onion, chopped
Dash dill
1/2 cup fresh mushrooms
1 cup orange juice
1 small salmon

Heat oven to 350°F. In large mixing bowl, combine dressing, butter, wine, onions, dill, mushrooms and orange juice; mix well. Place salmon on aluminum foil and fill cavity with stuffing mixture. Surround and top salmon with remaining stuffing. Top with orange slices. Fold foil around fish, place in pan and bake 1 hour.

Wayne Musilek
Sturgis, SD

Grilled
Salmon Rolls

Superb Salmon – Middle Eastern Style

Olive oil
Fresh skinless salmon fillets,
    cut into 2-inch slices
Fresh lemons, washed, halved
Salt
Pepper
Garlic powder
Ground cumin
Paprika
Carrots, thinly sliced
2 garlic cloves, sliced
Dried parsley

Generously grease 9-inch frying pan with olive oil, sides included. Rinse fillets and pat dry. Lay fillets on plate, outer side down. Squeeze generous amount of lemon over fillets and squeeze juice of 2 lemon halves into pan. Sprinkle fillets well with salt, pepper, garlic powder, cumin, and paprika. Place seasoned side down in pan. Repeat above seasonings on other side.

After seasoning, add carrots, and garlic. Liquid in the pan should be about half thickness of fish. Add water if necessary. Cover pan and bring to boil. Reduce heat and simmer 15 to 20 minutes. Add water as needed so fish does not dry out. Remove and place in casserole baking dish. Bake 20 to 30 minutes in 350°F oven, covered or uncovered, depending dryness preferred. Garnish with dried parsley.

Yaakov Kairy
Brooklyn, NY

Wickmaster Salmon

1 salmon fillet
1 (16-oz.) bottle Wishbone
    Italian Dressing
1/4 cup brown sugar

Heat oven to 350°F. Line baking sheet with foil, forming shallow dish to retain juices. Pour dressing into foil dish. Sprinkle brown sugar over fillet. Place fillet in aluminum foil. Bake 20 to 25 minutes. Let fillet stand for 10 minutes before serving.

Russ Franco
Yuba City, CA

Salmon Steaks with Creamy Sauce

2 salmon steaks, 1 inch thick
4 T. Dijon mustard
1/2 tsp. garlic powder
1 tsp. dried dill powder
1 T. lemon juice
3 T. white onion, finely chopped
1/2 cup reduced-calorie
mayonnaise
1 tsp. lemon juice
2 T. white wine
Paprika

Rinse steaks and pat dry. In large mixing bowl, combine mustard, garlic powder, dill and lemon juice; mix until well blended. Rub mixture onto fillets and smooth evenly. Refrigerate, covered, 2 hours. Meanwhile, combine onion, mayonnaise, lemon juice, white wine and paprika; mix well.

Cook steaks on hot grill until golden brown. Top with sauce.

Wayne Musilek
Sturgis, SD

Pickled Salmon

Salmon, skinned, boned and cut
   into 1- to 2-inch pieces
Pickling salt
1/2 gallon water
White vinegar
1 1/2 T. allspice
1 tsp. mustard seed
1/2 cup sugar
1/4 tsp. ginger
2 cups white vinegar
1/2 cup white port wine
White onion, sliced
1 lemon, sliced

Cover salmon in brine (3/4 cup pickling salt to 1/2 gallon water). Refrigerate 24 hours; drain. Cover salmon with white vinegar for 24; drain again. In large mixing bowl, combine allspice, mustard seed, sugar, ginger and vinegar; mix until well blended. Stir into stockpot; simmer mixture until sugar melts. Cool and add wine. Put drained fish in jars and alternate a layer of fish, white onion and lemon slices. Pour pickling mixture over fish. Refrigerate 10 days.

Wayne Musilek
Sturgis, SD

106

Old-Fashioned Salmon Patties

2 cups cooked salmon

2 eggs

2 cups soft bread crumbs

1/4 tsp. salt

1/8 tsp. pepper

1 small onion, chopped

2 T. lemon juice

Dry bread crumbs

1 T. grated Parmesan cheese

1/4 cup vegetable oil

In large mixing bowl, flake salmon with fork; beat in eggs. Add bread crumbs, salt, pepper, onion and lemon juice; mix well. Refrigerate about 30 minutes or more to set mixture. Form mixture into 8 to 10 patties. Dip into mixture of dry bread crumbs and cheese. In heavy skillet, heat oil over medium-high heat until hot. Drop patties into skillet and fry on both sides until brown and crisp.

Ray Kalisz
Battle Creek, M

Trout & Salmon

Salmon & Rice Balls

1 lb. canned salmon, flaked

1 cup cooked rice
   with 1/4 tsp. salt

2 eggs, beaten

1 T. onion, minced

1/2 cup bread crumbs

1/2 soup can of water

2 T. green pepper, chopped

1 (10 3/4-oz.) can cream
   of mushroom soup

Heat oven to 350°F. In large mixing bowl combine salmon, rice, eggs, onion and bread crumbs; mix until well combined. Form into balls. In another mixing bowl add water and green pepper to mushroom soup. Place sauce in shallow baking dish; drop salmon balls into sauce. Bake 30 minutes.

Joseph Sannino
Petersburg, NJ

Trout

Trout & Salmon

1 cup flour
1 tsp. salt
1 tsp. pepper
2 T. parsley
Dash cumin
4 trout fillets
2 eggs
Bread crumbs
Butter
Crushed pecans
2 T. Dijon or honey mustard
1/4 cup white wine
Parsley sprigs
Lemon, lime, tomato wedges

In large mixing bowl, combine flour, salt, pepper, parsley and cumin; mix until well blended. Dip fillets in mixture. In another mixing bowl, combine eggs and bread crumbs. Dip fillet in egg mixture; drain excess. In medium saucepan, heat butter over medium-heat until melted. Sauté fillets until light brown. Sprinkle with pecans. Sauté until nuts are lightly toasted. Mix mustard with wine. Spoon over trout; garnish with parsley sprig, small lemon, lime and tomato wedge. Serve with lightly sautéed baby snow peas and twice-baked potato.

Pedro Macias
Las Vegas, NV

Trout

Simple-Smoked Salmon Cheese Ball

1 (8-oz.) pkg. cream cheese, softened
1 cup finely chopped smoked salmon
¼ cup chopped white onion
1 T. liquid smoke
1 box Wheat Thins crackers

In large mixing bowl, combine cheese, salmon, onion and liquid smoke. Refrigerate several hours to harden. When cheese is hard, use wax paper to scoop cheese mixture out, and form ball. Place cheese ball on decorative plate. Surround with crackers and add sprig of parsley for color.

James Morris
Marysville, WA

Pecan-Smoked Rainbow Trout

2 rainbow trout fillets
1 cup lemon juice concentrate plus
2 T. Lemon juice
Lemon pepper
Black pepper

Start your smoker and load with 4 or 5 pieces of pecan wood. Put lemon juice concentrate into water pan with water. Lightly sprinkle trout with lemon juice. Sprinkle trout with lemon pepper and black pepper to taste. Smoke 1 to 1 1/2 hours.

Rich Pagel
Mechanicsburg, PA

Salmon Braised in Beer

2 lbs. salmon
1 T. butter
1 cup beer
1 bay leaf
1 tsp. peppercorns
1 carrot, sliced

Heat oven to 300°F. Place salmon in buttered casserole. Add beer, bay leaf, peppercorns and carrot. Cover with aluminum foil. Bake 20 minutes, or until fish flakes easily with fork.

Anonymous Member

Stuffed Lake Trout

Stuffed Lake Trout

1/2 cup butter
1 small onion, chopped
1 rib celery, sliced (about 1/2 cup)
4 cups bread cubes
1 tsp. sage or poultry seasoning
1 tsp. salt
1/2 tsp. pepper
4 T. parsley
1 lake trout

Heat oven to 375°F. In heavy skillet, heat butter over medium-high heat until melted. Sauté onions and celery. Add bread cubes, sage, salt, pepper and parsley. Toss lightly to mix well.

Meanwhile, place fish on foil covered baking sheet; stuff fish with vegetable mixture. Season with salt and pepper. Bake about 1 hour, depending on size of fish. Serve on lettuce leaves for fancy appearance.

Ronald Runyon
DuBois, PA

Trout & Salmon

Steelhead Trout

1 cup Teriyaki sauce
Steelhead fillets,
    cut into serving-size pieces
1 onion, sliced in rings
Seasoning salt
Pepper
1 tsp. lemon juice

Pour Teriyaki in large resealable plastic bag; add fillets and seal. Place in refrigerator 30 minutes. Wrap fillets in aluminum foil. Top with onion rings; season with salt and pepper. Add splash of lemon juice; fold foil tightly around fish. Cook over grill or broil in broiler about 3 to 4 minutes per side or until fish flakes. Cook, uncovered, 1 to 2 minutes.

Robert Frick
Johnstown, PA

Panfish

Cucumber Fish Salad

Cucumber Fish Salad

4 cucumbers, quartered,
  seeded, sliced
2 lbs. fish, poached, flaked
2 cups sour cream
1 pkg. dill dip mix
1 medium sweet pepper, diced
1 cup diced onion
2 jalapeño peppers, diced
2 ribs celery, sliced
1/2 cup diced dill pickles
4 medium tomatoes,
  seeded, diced
Salt and pepper

In large mixing bowl, combine cucumbers, fish, sour cream, dill dip, sweet pepper, onion, jalapeños, celery, pickles, tomatoes, salt and pepper; mix until well blended. Refrigerate 1 hour before serving.

Lewis Mosier
Sherwood, OH

Panfish

Crusty Perch

1 1/2 lbs. perch fillets
1/2 cup milk
1 cup cornflake crumbs
3 tsp. salt
4 tsp. olive oil

Heat oven to 400°F. In mixing bowl, pour 1/2 cup milk. In another mixing bowl, combine crumbs and salt. Dip fillets in milk and coat with crumb and salt mixture. Arrange fillets on well-greased baking sheet. Brush fillets with olive oil. Bake 15 minutes or until tender. Serve with lemon wedges or tartar sauce.

Ray Murley
Oshawa, Ont.

Beer Batter Fish

Vegetable oil
1 lb. fish fillets
3 to 4 T. baking mix plus 1 cup
1/2 tsp. salt
1 egg
3/4 cup beer

Heat 1 1/2 inches vegetable oil in deep fat fryer to 350°F. Cut fish into serving-size pieces. Lightly coat fillets with 3 to 4 tablespoons baking mix. In large mixing bowl, combine 1 cup baking mix, salt, egg and beer, mix until smooth. Dip fillets into mixture, letting excess drip into bowl. Fry, 2 minutes on each side, or until golden brown. Drain.

Thomas Reece
Porum, OK

Panfish

Panfish

1 lb. panfish fillets
2 eggs, beaten
2/3 cup Saltine crumbs
1/2 tsp. salt
Dash pepper
Vegetable oil

Rinse fillets and pat dry; cut into 4 serving-size pieces. In large mixing bowl, combine 2 eggs and 2 tablespoons water. In another mixing bowl combine Saltine crumbs, salt and pepper. Dip fish into egg mixture, then into crumb mixture. In heavy skillet, heat oil over medium-high heat until hot. Fry 5 to 6 minutes per side or until golden brown.

Seth Grantham
Bakersfield, CA

Country-Style Fish Chowder

1 qt. water
1 tsp. salt
4 large red potatoes
  (about 2 lbs.)
1 lb. lean panfish fillets
6 slices bacon, cut up
1 small onion, chopped
1/4 cup all-purpose flour
1/2 tsp. salt
1/8 tsp. pepper
1/8 tsp. dried thyme leaves
1 1/4 qts. milk
1 small bay leaf

In Dutch oven, bring water and salt to boil. Peel and chop potatoes into 1/2-inch cubes. Add potatoes to water; boil until tender. Drain and cool. Cut fillets into 1-inch pieces; set aside.

In heavy skillet, cook bacon until crisp. Remove and set aside. Add onion. Cook and stir until tender, about 2 minutes. Reduce heat.

In Dutch oven stir in flour, 1/2 teaspoon salt, pepper and thyme. Add bacon and onion. Blend in milk. Add bay leaf. Cook over medium heat, stirring constantly, until thickened and bubbly. Reduce heat to low. Stir in potatoes and fish. Cook over low heat, stirring gently, until fish flakes easily with fork, about 12 minutes. Garnish each serving with chopped chives, if desired.

Shane Felber
Kankakee, IL

Lemon-Fried Panfish

1 cup flour plus enough to coat
Juice of 1 lemon
2 tsp. salt
1/4 tsp. pepper
1 cup water
Vegetable oil
1 1/2 lbs. panfish

Heat oven to 375°F. In large mixing bowl combine flour, lemon juice, salt and pepper; mix until well blended. Stir in water; cover. Refrigerate 30 minutes. Heat 1 1/2 to 3 inches oil in deep fryer to 375°F. Coat fish with flour, then dip in chilled batter. Fry 3 minutes, turning occasionally, or until light golden brown. Drain on paper towels.

Eugene Starkey
McMinnville, TN

Mama's Deep Fry Fish

1 cup baking mix
1 1/2 tsp. seasoning salt
1 tsp. pepper
1/2 tsp. garlic powder
1/2 tsp. cayenne
1 1/2 lbs. skinless fillets, cut up
Peanut oil

In large mixing bowl, combine baking mix, salt, pepper, garlic and cayenne; mix until well blended. Coat fillets with dry mixture and deep fry in peanut oil at 375°F until golden brown.

Bill Fett
Cascade, MT

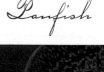

Perch

Perch fillets
1 egg, beaten
2 T. milk
Flour
Cornflake crumbs
Vegetable oil

Rinse fillets and dry on newspaper 10 minutes. In large mixing bowl, combine egg and milk. Dip fillets in flour, then egg and milk mixture. Before frying, dip in cornflake crumbs. Heat oil in heavy skillet over medium-high heat until hot. Fry fillets 4 to 5 minutes on each side.

Ray Murley
Oshawa, Ont.

Montana Fish Chowder

1/4 cup butter
1 T. flour
1 clove garlic, minced
1/2 cup chopped scallions
1/4 cup chopped green pepper
1/2 cup chopped celery
1/4 cup chopped zucchini
1 T. lemon juice
1/2 tsp. thyme
1/8 tsp. Tabasco sauce
1/2 tsp. salt
1/4 tsp. pepper
1 (15-oz.) can stewed tomatoes
1 1/2 lbs. skinless fillets, cut up

In heavy skillet, heat butter over medium-high heat until melted; whisk in flour. Add garlic, scallions, green pepper, celery and zucchini. When tender, add lemon juice, thyme, Tabasco, salt, pepper and stewed tomatoes. Simmer 45 minutes. Add fish and simmer an additional 2 to 3 minutes or until fish flakes.

Bill Fett
Cascade, MT

Panfish

Deep-Fried Perch Italiano

Drake's batter mix
Oregano
Garlic powder
Parmesan cheese
Perch fillets
Water or beer

In large mixing bowl, combine batter mix, oregano, garlic powder and Parmesan (season to taste); do not measure. Thin batter with water or beer. Dip fillets in batter. In heavy skillet, heat oil over medium-high heat until hot. Fry fillets until golden brown.

Mike Makowski
Saginaw, MI

Montana Fish Chowder

Deviled Fish

6 fish fillets
$^1/_4$ tsp. lime juice
$^1/_4$ cup plain yogurt
   or sour cream
$^1/_4$ cup mayonnaise
1 tsp. minced garlic
2 T. chopped onion
1 tsp. saffron powder
Salt and pepper
$^1/_2$ teaspoon prepared mustard
Parsley sprigs

Heat oven to 400°F. Arrange fillets in greased baking dish; sprinkle with lime juice. In large mixing bowl, combine yogurt, mayonnaise, garlic, onion, saffron powder, salt, pepper and mustard; mix until well blended. Spread mixture over fish. Bake 20 minutes. Garnish with parsley. Serve with white rice.

Kalowtie Seeriram
Queens, NY

Hawaii Diet Fish

Oil
Fish
Egg white
Cornmeal or crackers
Pineapple
Papaya
Macadamia nuts
Grated coconut

In large skillet, heat oil over medium-high heat until hot. Dip fish in egg white and then cornmeal or crackers. Place fillets in oil and fry until golden brown. Place fillets on platter and surround with fresh pineapple, papaya and macadamia nuts; sprinkle with grated coconut when ready to serve. Add small Jell-O or green salad with avocado for an easy-to-prepare complete meal. Maraschino cherries and seedless red grapes can be added for holiday color.

Elvira A. Switzer
Via Internet

Grilled Crappie

1 T. butter per fish
1 tsp. lemon juice per fish
1 tsp. Louisiana hot sauce
Crappie

In saucepan, heat butter over medium-high heat until melted; add lemon juice and hot sauce. Lay fish on foil. Pour sauce mixture over fish. Wrap fish and cook on hot grill until smoke rises. Turn and cook an additional 5 to 10 minutes or until fish is flaky.

Brad Caldwell
Winston, MO

Pecan-Coated Fried Fish

Pecan-Coated Fried Fish

2 eggs, beaten
1/4 tsp. salt
1/4 tsp. pepper
3/4 cup dry bread crumbs
3/4 cup ground pecans
cooking oil
2 lbs. skinless fillets
1/3 cup butter
1 T. lemon juice
1/4 tsp. cayenne

In large mixing bowl, combine eggs, salt and pepper; mix until well blended. In another bowl, mix bread crumbs and pecans. Dip fillets in egg mixture, then dredge in bread crumb mixture. In heavy skillet, heat oil over medium-high heat until hot. Fry fillets 5 to 8 minutes or until golden brown. In saucepan, heat butter, lemon juice and cayenne. Place fillets on serving platter and spoon sauce over fish.

Bill Fett
Cascade, MT

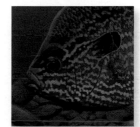

Fried Potato Fish

4 fish fillets
Salt and pepper
1 egg, beaten
Water
1 cup instant potato flakes
Cooking oil

Rinse fillets and pat dry. Season fillets with salt and pepper. In large mixing bowl, combine egg and water. Dip fillets in mixture, then dip in potato flakes. In heavy skillet, heat oil over medium-high heat until hot. Fry each fillet 4 to 5 minutes per side until golden brown. Drain on brown paper bag or paper towels.

Philip Bargeron
Harlem, GA

Foil-Baked Perch

2 lbs. perch fillets
1 (5-oz.) can condensed milk
1 cup finely ground bread crumbs
Lemon slice
Parsley sprigs

Heat oven to 500°F. Dip fillets in milk, then bread crumbs. Lay on oiled aluminum foil and bake 25 to 30 minutes. Garnish with lemon and parsley sprigs. Serve hot.

Ray Murley
Oshawa, Ont.

Panfish

Home-Fried White Perch

2 to 3 cups flour,
    depending on amount of perch
Ground pepper
1 T. Old Bay seasoning
White perch, cleaned
Oil
1/4 onion, chopped
1 to 2 sweet peppers, chopped
1 lemon
Dash pepper

In resealable plastic bag, mix flour, pepper and seasoning. Rinse perch and dip into mixture. Shake well to cover thoroughly. In heavy skillet, heat oil over medium-high heat until hot. Fry onion, sweet peppers and perch until golden brown. Serve with freshly squeezed lemon juice and dash of pepper.

Daniel & Jed Bessent & Dennis Baker
Elkton, MD

Fish & Cheese Chowder

2 T. butter
6 T. chopped onion
1 cup chopped carrots
6 T. chopped celery
1/4 cup flour
3 cups milk
2 (10 3/4-oz.) cans chicken broth
   or clam chowder
1 lb. fish fillets, cut into 1-inch
   pieces
1 cup grated cheese
1/2 tsp. salt
Dash paprika

In heavy skillet, heat butter over medium-high heat until melted; sauté onion, carrots and celery. In large mixing bowl, combine flour diluted with 1/2 cup milk; stir until smooth. Add to onion mixture. Combine mixtures in Dutch oven. Add remaining milk and broth. Cook, stirring constantly, until thickened. Add fish and simmer until fish flakes easily. Add cheese and stir until melted. Sprinkle with salt and paprika. Serve immediately.

Arnold McIntyre
Mayville, NY

Catfish

Fried Catfish

Fried Catfish

1 cup beer
1 cup flour
1 egg
Salt
6 catfish fillets
3 potatoes
Pepper

In large mixing bowl, combine beer, flour, egg and a pinch of salt in a bowl; mix well. Dip fillets in batter one at a time, let excess drain. In heavy skillet, heat oil over medium-high heat until hot. Fry fillets; drain and set aside. Peel and chop potatoes; add to remaining batter, along with pepper to taste. Drain with slotted spoon. Fry potatoes until light brown. Serve with fish.

Adam Stoltz
Jacobus, PA

Catfish Delight

2 catfish fillets
1 ½ cups clam sauce
Tabasco sauce

Marinate fillets in clam sauce for 1 hour; discard marinade. Wrap fillets loosely in foil and grill over hot coals until lightly browned. Sprinkle 3 drops of Tabasco sauce on each fillet.

Steven Stone
Tunkhannock, PA

Catfish with Fresh Corn Relish

4 (6-oz.) catfish fillets,
    1/2 inch thick
2 T. paprika
1/2 tsp. cayenne
1/2 tsp. salt

Catfish

Rinse fish and pat dry. In mixing bowl combine paprika, cayenne and salt; lightly sprinkle on both sides of fish. Grill fish on covered grill over medium charcoal briquets 5 to 9 minutes, turning once. (Grilling time depends on thickness of fish; allow 3 to 5 minutes for each 1/2 inch of thickness.) Serve with Fresh Corn Relish, lime wedges and grilled baking potatoes. Garnish with tarragon sprigs.

Fresh Corn Relish
1/4 cup cooked fresh corn
1/4 cup finely diced green bell pepper
1/4 cup finely slivered red onion
1 T. vegetable oil
2 T. (sweet) rice vinegar
Salt and pepper
1/2 cup quartered cherry tomatoes

In large mixing bowl, toss corn, green pepper, onion, oil and vinegar; mix well. Season with salt and pepper. Cover and refrigerate until ready to serve. Mix in tomatoes just before serving.

Michael Collins
Lenoir, NC

Poor Man's Fish Croquettes

Fresh fish fillets
Salt
Pepper
1 onion, chopped
1 sweet pepper, chopped
1 egg, well beaten
Cornmeal
Flour
Milk
Vegetable oil

Cut fish into sections about 4 to 6 inches long and cover with about 1 1/2 inches water in Dutch oven. Boil 30 to 45 minutes. Remove from heat; cool. Remove fillets. With fingertips, debone and skin fillets. Be sure to crumble well. In large mixing bowl, combine salt, pepper, onion, sweet peppers, egg, cornmeal, flour and milk; mix until well blended. Add enough milk to make medium-thin batter. Dip fillets in mixture. In heavy skillet, heat oil over medium-high heat until hot. Fry fillets until browned.

Jim Cushing
Graceville, FL

Grilled Catfish with Mango Salsa

Grilled Catfish with Mango Salsa

4 catfish fillets
2 tsp. olive oil
1 tsp. garlic salt
1/2 tsp. pepper
1/4 tsp. cayenne

Heat grill. Rinse fillets and pat dry. Brush each with 1/2 teaspoon oil. In large mixing bowl, combine garlic salt, pepper and cayenne; mix well. Sprinkle 1/2 teaspoon of mixture on rounded side of fillet. Grill over hot coals, rounded side down 3 to 4 minutes. Turn fillets over and grill an additional 3 to 4 minutes or until fish flakes easily when tested with a fork. Serve with mango salsa.

Mango Salsa

1 cup peeled, diced, mango
1 cup peeled, diced, papaya
1 T. minced green onion
1 T. minced red jalapeño pepper
2 T. fresh lime juice
1 T. honey

In large mixing bowl, combine mango, papaya, onion, pepper, juice and honey; mix well. Let sit at room temperature 20 minutes before serving.

Robert Patrick Black
Scranton, PA

Battered Catfish

1 (3-lb.) can shortening
2 eggs, beaten
1 cup milk
Salt and pepper
12 lbs. catfish, cut into steaks
Cornmeal

In saucepan, heat shortening over medium-high heat until melted. In large bowl, mix eggs and milk; salt and pepper fish, and dip into milk mixture. Roll fish in cornmeal. Drop fish into hot shortening. Fry until brown, turning once. Drain on absorbent paper.

Joseph Sannino
Petersburg, NJ

Catfish Cajun Style

1 1/2 lbs. potatoes
2 1/2 lbs. catfish fillets
1/4 tsp. salt
1/4 tsp. pepper
1/8 tsp. cayenne
1 tsp. paprika
1/4 tsp. thyme leaves
1/2 cup flour
4 T. peanut oil
2 T. butter
1 large clove garlic, minced
2 T. butter
1 tsp. lemon juice
Shredded sage leaves

Peel potatoes and cut into 2-inch sticks about 1/2 inch wide. Cut fish into same size as potatoes. Toss fish into resealable plastic bag with salt, pepper, cayenne, paprika, thyme and flour. Shake to coat all pieces; dump into colander to remove excess flour.

In heavy skillet, heat 2 tablespoons oil and 1 tablespoon butter over medium-high heat until hot. When hot, add fish in single layer and sauté 5 to 6 minutes until nicely browned.

Meanwhile, in another heavy skillet, heat remaining 2 tablespoons oil over medium-high heat until hot and 1 tablespoon butter until melted. Add potatoes; sauté until browned. Combine fish with potatoes. Add garlic and 2 tablespoons butter, toss well and place on platter. Add lemon juice and sage, if desired.

Paul H. Wells
Sierra Vista, AZ

Garlic-Fried Catfish

1 cup flour
1/2 cup buttermilk cornmeal
1/2 tsp. garlic powder
1/2 tsp. pepper
Salt
1/2 cup milk
2 cups vegetable oil
1 lb. fresh catfish fillets

In large mixing bowl, combine flour, cornmeal, garlic powder, pepper and salt; mix well. Place milk in separate bowl. In heavy skillet, heat oil over medium-high heat until hot. Slice fillets lengthwise in half; dip in milk. Dredge fillets in flour mixture; tap lightly to remove excess flour. Fry fillets until golden brown. Drain on paper towel.

Lance Poole
Lithia Springs, GA

Lemon-Baked Catfish

1 lemon
1 stick of butter
2 tsp. parsley
Salt and pepper
2 lbs. catfish fillets

Heat oven to 400°F. Grate rind off lemon into heavy saucepan. Squeeze lemon juice into saucepan. Add butter, parsley and salt and pepper. Heat until butter is melted. Place fish flat on baking sheet. Pour mixture over each fillet. Bake 15 minutes or until fish flakes easily with a fork.

Nancy Newton
Houston, TX

Grilled Catfish with Citrus Marinade

¹/₄ cup orange juice
2 T. vegetable oil
2 T. light soy sauce
1 T. lemon juice
1 tsp. garlic, minced
¹/₈ tsp. pepper
4 catfish fillets

In large mixing bowl, combine orange juice, oil, soy sauce, lemon juice, garlic and pepper; mix until well blended. Place catfish fillets in a 13 x 9 x 2-inch dish; add marinade. Cover and marinate 3 hours. Heat oven to 450°F. Remove fish from marinade. Arrange fillets on greased baking pan. Bake 8 to 10 minutes or until done.

Erick Long
Camdenton, MO

Catfish

Mustard-Fried Catfish

Peanut oil
Hot mustard
Tabasco sauce
1 clove garlic, minced
Salt and pepper
2 lbs. catfish fillets
Yellow cornmeal

In heavy skillet, heat oil over medium-high heat until hot. In resealable plastic bag, combine mustard, Tabasco, garlic, salt and pepper; shake to mix well. Add fillets and marinate 4 hours. Discard marinade; coat fillets in cornmeal. Fry fillets in oil until golden brown.

Justin Williamson
Tucson, AZ

Bass

Cajun-Style Sea Bass

Cajun-Style Sea Bass

2 tsp. dried oregano

2 tsp. sweet paprika

1/2 tsp. ground ginger

1/2 tsp. pepper

1/4 tsp. cayenne

1 T. olive oil

4 thick sea bass steaks

Salt

Thyme

Lemon peel, slivered

In large mixing bowl, combine oregano, paprika, ginger, pepper, cayenne and oil; rub over steaks to coat. In heavy skillet, heat oil over medium-high heat 2 minutes. Add steaks, smooth side down; fry 2 to 3 minutes, until just beginning to blacken. Turn steaks over, reduce heat and cook an additional 3 to 6 minutes. Sprinkle with salt, thyme and lemon just before serving.

Anthony G. Andrews, Jr.
Lebanon, NY

Bass

Basic Fish Fry

Fish fillets

Salt

Pepper

Cornbread mix

Vegetable oil

Rinse fillets and pat dry. Season with salt and pepper. Pour cornbread mix into mixing bowl; dip fillets. In heavy skillet, heat oil over medium-high heat until hot. Fry fillets until browned. Drain on brown paper bags or paper towels.

Philip Bargeron
Harlem, GA

Parmesan Bass Fillets

1 1/2 lbs. bass, about 3/4 inch thick
1/4 cup butter
1/8 tsp. salt
1/8 tsp. pepper
1 T. fresh lemon juice
1 T. white wine
3 T. grated Parmesan cheese
Paprika

Heat oven to 450°F. Cut fish into serving-size pieces. Place butter in 13 x 9-inch baking pan; place in oven 5 minutes to melt butter. Place fish in pan, skin side up. Sprinkle with salt and pepper. Bake 5 minutes, turn over. Sprinkle with lemon juice and white wine. Top with Parmesan cheese. Sprinkle with paprika. Bake 5 minutes, or until fish flakes easily with fork.

Eugene Starkey
McMinnville, TN

Bass

Stuffed Baked Bass

3 T. butter
1/2 cup finely chopped celery
1 cup finely chopped small onion
1/2 cup sliced mushrooms
1/2 cup uncooked rice
2 T. lemon juice
1/2 tsp. dill weed
1/8 tsp. thyme
Salt and pepper
3 to 5 lbs. bass,
Fresh parsley

Heat oven to 350°F. In heavy skillet, heat butter over medium-high heat until melted. Sauté celery, onion and mushrooms about 7 minutes. In saucepan, cook rice according to directions and drain. Toss rice with vegetables, lemon juice, dill weed, thyme and salt and pepper to taste. Butter one side of aluminum foil and place in baking dish. Stuff fish with rice mixture. Close opening with skewers and lace with heavy string.

Place fish on foil, cover and bake 50 to 60 minutes or until fish flakes easily with fork. Remove foil packet from baking dish; place on heated serving dish. Garnish with parsley and serve.

John Pelrine
Chicago, IL

152

Smoked Bass

Bass fillets
8 oz. cheddar cheese
Freshly ground pepper
Garlic powder
Mushrooms
Almonds
1 medium onion,
   chopped

Utilizing water smoker, use full pan (10 lbs.) hardwood charcoal and several handfuls of hickory chips soaked in water 6 hours. After coals are gray, add hot water to water pan and two handfuls of hickory chips. Smoke fillets 2 to 4 hours, or until they flake with fork.

Place cheese in aluminum foil pan. Sprinkle pepper and garlic powder to taste; smoke 1 1/2 hours. Put whole mushrooms on grill and smoke 1 hour. Put almonds in aluminum foil and smoke 1 hour (salt lightly, if desired). Add new coals and more hickory chips as needed.

Slice medium onion 3/4 inch thick and smoke an additional 1 1/2 to 2 hours. Top fillets with cheese, mushrooms, almonds and onion.

Randy Jacobs
Lubbock, TX

Edd's Bass Salad

Bass

2 (8-oz.) cooked fillets,
  cubed
Lemon juice
1 tsp. paprika
1 tsp. seasoning salt
Fresh parsley sprigs
$^1/_4$ cup white vinegar
$^1/_2$ cup oil
$^1/_4$ cup water
$^1/_4$ cup cubed tomatoes
$^1/_4$ cup cubed cucumbers
$^1/_4$ cup chopped olives
$^1/_2$ cup thinly sliced turnips
$^1/_2$ cup thinly sliced red onion
1 tsp. salt
1 tsp. pepper
4 cups cooked pasta

In large mixing bowl, combine cooked fillets, lemon juice, paprika, seasoning salt and parsley sprigs; mix until well blended. In another mixing bowl, combine vinegar, oil and water with tomatoes, cucumber, olives, turnips, onion, salt and pepper; toss. Combine mixtures, toss with pasta. Serve salad hot or cold the following day.

Edd McCannon
Lingnall, GA

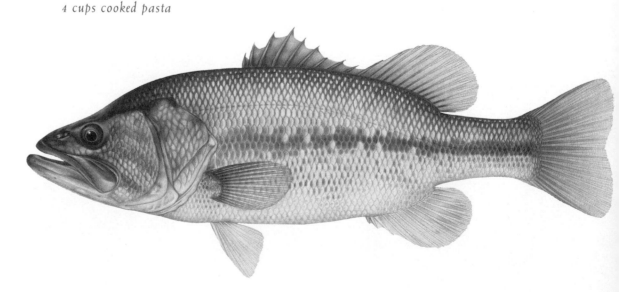

Edd's Bass Salad

Bubba's Bass Recipe

¹/₂ to 1 tsp. Old Bay seasoning
¹/₂ to 1 tsp. Italian seasoning
¹/₂ to 1 tsp. garlic salt or powder
Dash salt and pepper
2 eggs
¹/₂ cup milk
3 T. butter
1 to 2 lbs. bass, filleted
Italian bread crumbs
1 lemon, sliced

Heat oven to 350°F. In large mixing bowl, combine seasonings, eggs and milk; mix well. Rub fillets with butter, lightly dip into batter, and sprinkle with bread crumbs. Arrange fillets on sheet of foil; wrap like tent, not touching sides and top of fish. Place remaining butter in packet, if desired. Top with lemon slice. Bake 10 to 15 minutes until fish is cooked through.

Ken Gallagher II
Centreville, VA

Black Bass in Onion Soup

2 lbs. large bass fillets
Salt and pepper
Garlic powder
1 pkg. prepared onion soup mix
1 cup white wine
Paprika

Heat oven to 350°F. Wash fillets and pat dry. Arrange fillets on large piece of aluminum foil. Season with salt, pepper and garlic powder. Turn edges of foil to make a bowl. Add soup mix, pour in wine and sprinkle generously with paprika. Bake 1 1/2 to 2 hours or until fish flakes easily with fork.

John Pelrine
Chicago, IL

Bass

Striped Bass

Striped bass
Butter
2 medium onions,
    cut up
2 small green bell peppers,
    cut up

Heat oven to 400°F. Coat fish in butter. Arrange fish in aluminum foil. Top with onions and green peppers. Wrap tightly. Bake 30 minutes.

Frances & Ethan Freeman
Arbuckle, CA

Index